Finding Your Financial Path

A guide for women through life's twists and turns

Stuart Vick Smith

Stuart Vick Smith
ML&R Wealth Management LLC
401 Congress, Suite 1100
Austin, TX 78701
www.stuartvicksmith.com

Printed in the United States of America.

For Steve, Mackenzie and Whit.
I have loved all of our twists, turns and mountain climbs.

Contents

Preface

I've always loved numbers.

I remember visiting my dad's office during the summers and playing on the ten-key adding machine. How many 10-year-old kids do you know who actually like to add up numbers for fun?

That was me.

My love for numbers carried over to the world of money. I always insisted on being the banker in Monopoly and loved my first job as a checker at the local grocery store. My college job as a teller at a bank was a dream come true – money everywhere. I liked stacking the coins, counting the bills and thinking of all the possibilities. I was hooked from the very beginning.

I remember how excited I was to have my first real job out of graduate school. When I paid my bills each month, I felt like I was really accomplishing something special.

I felt pride and satisfaction watching my first retirement account grow with each new contribution and seeing the investment returns add to the balance.

With my love for numbers and money, my career took me to the tax profession, and later to the investment field with a focus on women and their wealth. When I first started as an investment advisor, I quickly realized that the industry did little to meet the needs of women.

Women were being ignored, underserved, even patronized. Basically, women were not given the time or the opportunity to participate in their own financial futures.

Fighting the stereotypes

Many people, including some women, believe that money is male territory. This bias tells us that women aren't well suited to making it, managing it or investing it. Fortunately, my parents taught me differently. They taught me that women can (and do) work as hard as men, have the right to earn as much as men and are smart and disciplined enough to manage their money as well as men.

Through my practice, I've had the good fortune to work with many amazing women, often in the wake of challenging life events – whether it is the death of their spouse, divorce or helping their aging parents. These events thrust them, sometimes with no warning, into a new and unfamiliar role as financial decision maker.

In these difficult situations, my goal as an advisor is always to educate, inform and help women land on their feet prepared to take on the world, or at a minimum, confidently oversee their own money and investments.

This book centers on these life transitions with the hope of outlining advice to help every woman find financial comfort and security, no matter what situation she encounters or how she got there.

Jargon-free zone

As your read, you'll notice something unusual about this book – there are no charts or graphs, no Venn diagrams or time sequences, no historical patterns or future predictions. While the topic is financial, the presentation is plain English, no jargon. There are many great financial books available, each full of carefully plotted graphs and elaborate asset allocation diagrams. Unfortunately, I don't believe they get to the heart of what is important to women.

In creating ***Finding Your Financial Path***, I made a commitment to produce a book that could be read quickly and understood easily. This is not meant to be a finance textbook. This is a practical guide for any woman who needs to take control of her financial life. I hope you find it useful as you work your way through your own twists and turns to reach the long-term financial stability you desire and deserve.

Keep in mind that this book is not intended as a replacement for professional advice related to your own unique circumstances. Instead, it should help you understand your situation and know what kind of questions to ask if you do work with a financial advisor.

Changing Roles

1

The Shift of Wealth to Women

Prepare for the responsibility of managing wealth.

When it comes to finances in America, women have historically been relegated to the back seat. Our grandmothers typically received little financial guidance from their parents, and once married, relied on their husbands to manage the investments and checkbook.

This second-class status needs to change, and it is changing. This chapter explores the shift in American wealth and what it means for women.

A Reversal of Fortunes

In recent decades, women have gained more control over the family finances, perhaps managing the household budget or paying some of the bills. Still, in most families, men have made the big financial decisions, with or without the input of women.

This longstanding bias extends to the investment business as well. I can assure you that when I attend professional conferences for advisors, very few attendees are women.

Here comes the money

Times are changing. In the next decade, women are expected to control roughly two-thirds of the total spending power in the United States. We have come a long way, baby!

But it's not just spending power. Women are also going to be more in charge of their own wealth. A dramatic shift of wealth from men to women is underway. Why?

Life expectancy is a big component. Statistics show that, on average, women outlive men by five years. With many baby boomers now in their 60s, more and more widows are taking over the family finances. Because of the differential in longevity, a substantial portion of baby-boomer wealth will pass into the hands of women in coming years.

In many families, this will be the first time the wife has taken the lead on investments and family finances.

Divorce contributes to the shift as well. With a divorce rate approaching 50 percent, more and more women are independently managing their own money. And because divorced women are less likely to remarry than divorced men, they may remain in full control of their own wealth for the rest of their lives.

Here's another demographic fact: In younger generations, women are waiting longer to get married. It's more common today for a woman to establish her own career and buy a home before tying the knot. I also see more and more women keeping their finances separate after they get married.

Finally, many women in their 30s and 40s are experiencing faster career tracks and higher earnings than previous generations. This trend means more independent wealth for women than ever before.

Taking Responsibility

Each of these demographic events will cause a movement of money and investments to women. With all of them happening at once, we must expect a tsunami of wealth transfers from men to women.

Women currently control 39 percent or $11 trillion dollars of investable assets in the U.S. It is predicted that another $28 trillion of wealth will transfer to women over the next 40 years.

> Ninety percent of women will be directly responsible for their finances at some point in their lifetime.

With this coming change, women must get ready. It's time for women to expand their financial knowledge and be more involved in their own finances. Women need to be prepared to excel in the role of financial leader and steward of their family's assets.

When you think about it, it's not just our own financial well-being at stake; it's the financial future of the country as well. It is time for us to step up and take charge. Reading this book is a small, strong step in that direction.

2

The Investment Gap

It's time to catch up.

You don't need me to tell you that women continue to struggle for equality on many levels. Financially, we face an uphill battle to land the best jobs and earn an equal wage.

Women also face a dramatic disadvantage in investing for long-term goals, especially retirement. This chapter looks at causes of this disadvantage and how to overcome them.

It's Not Just a Wage Gap

As a Generation X'er, I grew up in the era of women's lib and saw an increasing number of women entering the workforce. (Way to go, Mom!) I know many women who have risen to the top of their professions.

But overall, we're still playing catch-up financially.

The wage gap – women earning less than men – is well known. But that's not the only disadvantage women face financially. There's also a significant *investment gap* between men and women in our country. This gap challenges women as they seek to build assets to fund retirement.

To bridge the gap, we must first understand the reasons behind it and then take intentional steps to change the direction of investing for women.

How did we get here?

This investment gap is a product of both societal norms and behavioral differences between men and women. (Remember Venus vs. Mars?)

The investment gap begins with compensation. As we all know, women in the U.S. earn about 77 cents on the dollar, on average, compared to men. Because women earn less than men, they have less to save for retirement.

In addition to lower wages, women are more likely to take time off, reduce their work schedule or opt for a less demanding (and lower paying) job during child-rearing years. Therefore, the wage gap widens for many women while they raise their families.

As these compensation differences play out over a full career, women typically put away for retirement only about two-thirds as much as their male counterparts.

An unhappy aside

Lower earnings may mean lower Social Security benefits as well, adding another layer of cash flow issues during retirement.

The Danger of Safety

The investment gap is compounded by another factor. Basically, women behave differently when it comes to investing.

Women are generally more risk-averse with their money than men. As a group, women prefer "safer," less volatile investments.

Unfortunately, reducing risk in a portfolio also reduces its expected return.

Everyone understands the dangers of taking too much risk in investing – such as betting all your savings on an unknown tech startup – but taking too little risk can be dangerous, too.

So-called safer investments, such as bonds instead of stocks, can lead to very low returns that barely beat inflation and do little to build portfolio balances for the long term.

Earn less, live longer

And finally, women live, on average, five years longer than men. The money in a woman's portfolio is not only a third less than a man's; it also has to last five years longer.

Taken together, lower pay, reduced work hours, aversion to risk and a longer life expectancy severely limit the retirement income available to a woman. This reduced income will significantly impact her lifestyle throughout retirement – meaning she may need to work longer or spend significantly less in retirement than her male counterpart.

Close the Gap

Women face real challenges related to building wealth. But they're not insurmountable. Many women can and do manage their money successfully and enjoy financial security.

I've found in working with women for many years that the most important step to getting on the right track is education. The more you know about money, the greater confidence you will have about your future and the better equipped you'll be to make financial decisions for yourself and your family.

More knowledge will also help you find the right kind of advisor to assist you on more complex financial matters.

Control what you can

You may not have control over the wage gap for the entire female population, but you can control how your own portfolio is invested. You can control whether it is aligned with your long-term goals. You can control some factors that influence your taxes. You can control your investment costs so that you keep more of what you make.

While it's easy to procrastinate on financial matters, closing the investment gap should be a priority throughout your career. Just like saving, the sooner you start, the more progress you can make toward long-term financial stability.

Life's Transitions

3

Partners in Love, Life and Money

Commit to communicate about finances.

Few things in life are more satisfying and exhilarating than finding that special someone with whom to spend your life. But marriage is much more than a spiritual and emotional union; it is also a merger of households, families and finances.

This chapter shares important matters to consider and discuss if you are a newlywed or about to become one.

Have the Conversation

Let's be honest. Money is one of the last things couples want to discuss.

Talking about money can be stressful. It may seem too private a matter to discuss out loud. You may feel embarrassed about financial mistakes you've made, or you may just not know much about the subject. Discussing finances with your partner may reveal differences that are difficult to reconcile.

And that's the whole point. That's why you need to talk about it.

Money is one of the most reliable causes of stress and conflict in a marriage. You need to be able to talk openly and rationally with your partner about finances to avoid surprises and disagreements. I strongly encourage you to start talking about money before you go down the aisle, whether it is your first marriage or a return trip.

Start with the facts

Money can be very emotional, so I suggest you and your partner start this important conversation with facts about your current situation:

- Do you have savings, investments or money put away for retirement?
- Do you have student loans, credit card balances or other debt?
- What are your income and spending like?
- Do you follow a budget?

- Do you help support your parents, adult children, or other family members?
- Do you have any other assets or liabilities that you've not previously discussed?
- How is your credit?

The goal of this conversation is to avoid surprises in the future. Complete two-way candor is essential.

If all this financial disclosure seems a little too invasive, remember that in marriage your finances will be tied together, even if you keep some accounts separate. Your personal credit rating will be affected by the actions of your spouse. You really do need to know what he or she brings to the marriage, both positive and negative. And vice versa.

Know where you stand

Discussing these facts will help you get on the same page regarding some financial basics for your marriage. For instance:

- If you have outstanding student loans, will they be your responsibility to pay off, or will you work on it together?
- Will you build savings in joint accounts or individually?
- If you come to the marriage with a house and a mortgage, will you both contribute to the payments and maintenance?
- Who owns the house – you alone or you and your spouse?

Get Emotional

The next phase of the conversation is the emotional side of money.

Everyone comes from different backgrounds – different family situations, careers, cultures, religions, and political viewpoints. These differences shape our values and priorities, including those related to money.

> Personal history matters, too. How money was handled in your family can have a big influence on the rest of your life.

For instance, think of people you know who grew up in the Great Depression and are still influenced by that experience 70 years later.

With these differences in mind, talk with your mate about how each of you think about money:

- What does money mean to you?
- What major goals do you have related to money?
- If money were scarce, what would your priorities be?
- What are your fears related to money?
- Are you more of a spender or a saver?
- How important are material things, such as a luxurious home or expensive car?
- If you were wealthy, how would you want to live?
- On what kinds of things do you like and dislike spending money?

There are no right or wrong answers to these questions, but the answers will help you understand how your spouse feels.

As you combine households and finances, this conversation will put choices and decisions into context, and establish a basis for future conversations about money.

To avoid surprises, have this conversation early on. If your spouse has a dream to build an incomparable collection of rare cars, it is better to learn about this desire early in the relationship than to find out he has cashed in his 401k plan and left for the classic car auction.

Where are We Going?

There's one more layer of communication about money and marriage: your goals and plans for the future.

Although everyone comes into a marriage with grand ideas of a long and happy life together, what does that really mean for you and your partner? What are the specifics that will make your life together rewarding and meaningful?

Family

What does your ideal family look like, and how will you get there?

> You may both want children, but you may disagree on the details.

Your spouse may want to get started on a large family right away, while you prefer to focus on your career for a time, build up your savings and have fewer children. This can be a tricky conversation, but it has important implications, including financial ones.

Career

Will both of you work, and if so, for how long? Some people start counting down in their 30s to the day they can retire. Others look forward to working forever. Where do you and your spouse fall on this spectrum?

While an investment strategy is extremely important, your most valuable long-term asset is your ability to work and earn money. How long you work and what kind of job you have will have a major impact on how you live in retirement.

Experiences

Many studies show that experiences (trips, events, time with loved ones, etc.) are more valuable and memorable than material goods.

What experiences do you look forward to, and when will you pursue them? If travel is a priority for you and your spouse, do you want to put away money now for future adventures, or would you rather do all the travel you can while you are younger, leaving less money for your retirement years?

Questions like these can have a big influence on how you earn, save and spend your money. Sharing and comparing ideas with your partner will help you work together for your mutual happiness.

Solo or Joint?

When I got married, there wasn't any money, so whatever we earned went into a joint account. As we got older and our finances got a little more complex, we added separate accounts and paid ourselves an allowance so we had freedom over our own discretionary spending.

This arrangement gave us the ability to manage household bills while not requiring joint decision-making over every single dollar spent. It worked for us.

I've seen many younger couples keep their finances separate for the most part, and share household expenses by divvying up the bills.

Others throw all the money in a joint account and everything is shared equally.

You need to determine what feels right for you and your spouse.

> What you want to avoid is any scenario where either partner feels like he or she is being treated unfairly or has a lesser say in the family's financial decisions.

Also think about short- and long-term investments. Will you pool your resources for retirement, college costs and other big expenses? Think about your goals and how they come together as a couple; this will help you determine the most comfortable and convenient way to set up your investment accounts. An investment advisor can help you sort out your options.

For more money tips for couples, see Chapter 14, "I Thought You Paid that Bill..."

Do We Need a Prenup?

There, I said it.

Just saying the words "prenuptial agreement" can trigger strong emotions and potential conflicts. Regardless of how you frame the discussion, raising the topic ultimately means you are thinking about the possibility that the marriage will fail.

Like it or not, prenuptial agreements do have their time and place. No matter how strong your mutual commitment is today, things can change. And for about half the married couples in the U.S., they do change.

> Consider what you want to protect if your marriage doesn't last.

Whether you have assets from a prior marriage, an inheritance from a family member or an investment portfolio you built on your own, you should understand your options for protecting them.

Likewise, if you are planning to give up your career to raise children, you may want some assurances about your financial well-being if the marriage dissolves.

Consult an attorney to get a better idea of what it would mean to have an agreement in place, as well as the risks associated with not having one.

By the same token, if your fiancé suggests a prenup, be sure to consult an attorney for your own protection.

In marriage, as in most aspects of life, transparency and communication go a long way to prevent and solve problems. Candid discussion of financial topics before you get married can save a lot of trouble down the road.

4

When Happily is Not Ever After

Protect your financial interests in a divorce.

Although divorce has become commonplace in American society, it is rarely easy. Even in the most amicable divorces, both parties must deal with decisions and changes that would have seemed unimaginable during happier times.

Here are some starting points.

On Your Own Does Not Mean Alone

Spouses grow into partners that work together to create a household, earn money and build wealth. Joint decisions are made about the household, kids and finances. Priorities and goals are developed together, as a team.

But. Then.

In divorce, that intense and satisfying collaboration comes to an abrupt, and sometimes contentious, end. Suddenly, your whole world looks different.

> It can feel confusing, depressing or scary to be on your own. Especially when it comes to money.

While you may find it difficult to trust others as you set out on your own, assembling a team of advisors should be an absolute priority.

I'm not talking about good friends and relatives who care about you and want to help, although these people are important too.

I'm not talking about your recently divorced college friend who claims to know everything there is to know on the subject.

I'm talking about professionals who have worked with divorcees many times. I'm talking about impartial experts who can answer questions you don't even know you need to ask.

Your team

Of course, you'll need an attorney to clarify your legal options and pursue whatever strategy you choose. But you'll also need other advisors to lean on throughout the process.

An accountant can help with tracking and finding your assets. Specialized appraisers may be needed to help value a family business or other unique assets. A realtor can help with property valuations.

Finally, a financial advisor can help you understand where you are financially and chart a path forward.

Once you have assembled your team of experts, you can take a deep breath knowing you are not alone.

How to find the experts you need

Your advisors are important to your future. Take the time to do some research:

- Start with recommendations from friends, family and other trusted advisors
- Check local professional organizations in the field
- Confirm the individuals have the appropriate professional credentials
- Interview top candidates to make sure they are a good fit

Yours. Mine. Ours.

Your next priority will be to assess what you have – both as individuals and jointly.

This inventory process will mean looking at physical and financial assets in a new way, assigning them to the proper column – yours, mine, ours – and determining fair market values.

Start with the basics and then go deeper.

- The house
- Other real estate
- Checking and savings accounts
- Investment accounts
- Retirement accounts
- Family businesses
- Jewelry
- Fine art
- Furnishings
- Automobiles
- Club memberships
- Personal property

Check the math

Whether you create this inventory with or without the cooperation of your spouse, it is up to you to be sure it's complete and fair. Don't take your spouse's list at face value.

When confirming financial assets, keep in mind that an estimated 7.2 million adults have hidden a bank account or credit card from their spouse at some point in their marriage.

It's also known to happen that a spouse will conceal, divert or misrepresent the cash flow of a family business. An accountant (sometimes a specialist called a forensic accountant) can investigate to identify any assets or income that have not been fully disclosed. Your attorney can help you decide if this is necessary and worth the expense.

Assigning values to some assets can be tricky. The value of a savings or retirement account is pretty straightforward.

But what about that painting of the blue dog?

The one you bought 30 years ago from the then unknown artist George Rodrigue? Consider getting appraisals for rare and unique pieces like this.

It's Not Just Things

The inventory of physical and financial assets can be a big job. You'll also need to think about assigning expenses.

Who will have financial responsibility for the house, the children, education, insurance and other expenses? Who will repay any debts? And don't forget the pets; their care can be expensive.

There will also be new expenses. For instance, when you or your spouse moves to a new residence, there will be a mortgage or rent, plus maintenance, utilities, and so on.

Even though it may be the last thing you want to think about, early in the divorce process you should make a budget that reflects your new reality. What will it cost – really cost – to live the life you want?

This may all seem like a lot of aggravating math. That's fair. But it's math with a purpose.

The divorce settlement process relies on accurate numbers for what you have, what you need, and who will be responsible for what.

The importance of this assessment process cannot be overstated. If the numbers aren't valid and complete, the division of assets, expenses and responsibilities may be inequitable, leaving you in a difficult financial situation.

Take the time to get it right.

Deal-Breakers and Must-Haves

You might begin the divorce journey with only a vague final destination in mind:

- Whatever is best for the kids
- A fair, equitable settlement
- Financial independence

These are completely valid ideas, but as you move forward in the process you'll find that you need to be more specific about what these goals mean.

What do you want your new life to look like?

Make a list and rank the most important goals, so you know where to focus your time and energy. Do you want to:

- Stay in the house? Move out? Move away?
- Keep the kids in their home?
- Have sole or shared custody?
- Fully fund college?
- Quit your job? Change careers? Go back to work?
- Go back to school?
- Downsize and simplify?
- Retain the vacation home?
- Provide care for aging parents?

Which are most important? Which are absolute must-haves? Where can you compromise?

Lean on your professional advisors for help and guidance as you translate these priorities into specific elements of the divorce decree.

Back on Your Own Two Feet

If you've ever done an extensive home remodel, you'll probably recall the demolition phase. You walk into your home and find it in a shocking state of chaos and dust. You feel disoriented. You wonder if it will ever feel like a home again.

Having worked with many women going through divorce, I know you may have that same feeling now, like you have taken a big and uncomfortable step backward.

It's against this unsettling backdrop that you must look forward. Visualize where you want to be – whether it is one year, five years or ten years from now.

Start building toward that vision.

Make changes that reinforce your independence and enable you to take control of your own destiny.

> If big steps seem too daunting, start small.

Establish a new budget.

Set up your savings plan and be diligent in making contributions.

Monitor and adjust your plan along the way to make sure you stay on track.

Talk to your financial advisor about what you have now, your sources of future income, and how best to invest those assets to create a life where you once again feel comfortable, safe and happy.

Just as your home remodel was eventually finished and better than ever, with planning, discipline and support from your professional experts, you can get through this. And you will.

5

Hard Work Pays Off

Have a plan when you sell your business.

Women make excellent entrepreneurs. We have a genuine passion for what we do, and we're not afraid of hard work. Though it often entails blood, sweat and tears, our efforts can result in thriving and valuable businesses.

Selling your business marks a huge milestone, both financially and emotionally. This chapter explores some of the issues that you should consider before, during and after the sale.

More Than a Career

The number of women-owned companies in the U.S. continues to climb. Women own 9.4 million enterprises, more than 30 percent of all businesses in the country.

Women entrepreneurs generate jobs, foster innovation and inspire girls to pursue their dreams. And for many women, entrepreneurship has another result: *wealth.*

I work with many women who are selling their businesses or planning to do so. While each woman is driven by her own goals – whether it is a new lifestyle, a different career or retirement – our discussions tend to revolve around several key ideas.

What's your plan?

Just as you created a business plan when you started your venture, make a plan for when and how you will sell it.

Perhaps you plan to sell when the company's value reaches a certain level. Or the timing may be based on your age or family needs. Or you may have more career ideas to explore as a serial entrepreneur.

Whatever your circumstances, approach the sale realistically.

> It's natural to see your own business as the best and most valuable, but its true value is what a buyer is willing to pay.

A potential buyer, without the emotional attachment you have to the business, may not place the same value on your products, reputation, location or clientele.

You'll need to justify your selling price with facts. Do the research and determine the dominant valuation metrics for your industry. Purchase prices in your field may be a multiple of revenue, net profit or some other measure. These are the numbers prospective buyers care about, so track them regularly to develop a valid idea of your company's value.

I suggest you speak to owners of similar companies to see what they experienced when buying or selling.

Keep saving

As you build your business toward the exit point, make sure you are saving for retirement. A common mistake entrepreneurs make is to put every dime into their companies. This creates a dangerous double threat: If the business fails, you lose not only your livelihood, but also your nest egg.

Plan to take some money off the table each year and build your portfolio. This assures that not all of your assets are at risk in your company. As net income grows, take more money out and diversify it across other investments.

If you're not able to pull money out of the business on a regular basis, you may need to re-evaluate. It will be very difficult to sell a business that can't demonstrate consistently strong positive cash flow.

Get Your House in Order

We all know that selling a neat, orderly house in good condition is far easier than selling one that's full of clutter or falling apart. The same principle applies to selling a business.

> You will want your business to be at its absolute best before it goes on the market.

Take the time to get everything in tip-top shape. For starters:

- Make sure your company is running efficiently and effectively
- Keep software and technologies up-to-date
- Document all contracts with clients, vendors and suppliers and keep them current
- Clean up your finances and keep your books and taxes in spotless condition
- Get the right people on board to move your company forward
- Make sure all legal documents are current and available

Tell your story

Put together a clear and compelling presentation or proposal to have available for interested parties. Anticipate the questions a buyer will have and be ready with the answers. Make it easy for the potential buyer to see the value your company provides.

As prospects move closer to an offer, be ready for an extensive due diligence process. Your job is to make that process as easy and straightforward as possible.

Involve the experts

Even if you are the best CEO and lead the top company in your industry, you are probably not an expert at selling a business. Don't make the mistake of doing it yourself to save a few dollars. Get professional help.

Hire an attorney who is experienced in business sales and acquisitions. She can help you determine the appropriate structure for the sale and protect your interests throughout the process.

Include accountants on your team of advisors. You will want to have auditors to help during the due diligence phase, and tax accountants to determine the best structure from a tax standpoint.

Also consider the benefit of engaging a broker to help you find the right buyer. Though brokers take a cut of the deal, they bring value to the table.

> A broker can greatly expand the universe of qualified buyers and may be able to secure a higher selling price.

Finally, make sure to consult with your investment advisor along the way. If you have the sale of your business in your long-term plan, make sure that the expected outcome aligns with your goals. For instance, if you originally expected to sell your business for two million dollars and now find it will sell for only half of that, discuss with your advisor the impact on your long-term financial situation.

Look Beyond the Deal

Before the sale, think about how – if at all – you want to stay involved in the business.

Some sellers stay on full time for months or years. Others may act as a consultant to help the transition go smoothly. And some happily walk away after signing the final documents.

The buyer will have thoughts about whether and how you stay involved, but decide what you prefer in advance and make that clear during the sales process.

As you consider your options, think about the implications for yourself, both financial and emotional.

Depending on the selling price and the structure of the payout, it may be difficult to step away from your paycheck. You may need to transition into your next phase of life by working part time or consulting for the new owner.

> Because you know more about the business than anyone else, you may be able to negotiate a relatively high salary or consulting fee.

The emotional side of the decision can be more complex. If you decide to stay involved, know that you will no longer be the ultimate decision-maker. The new owner may make changes that do not sit well with you. She may not treat your old customers and employees the way you did.

You may find it stressful to take a back seat in the business you built yourself. Be prepared for this change if you plan to stay on.

Make the payout pay off

Many sales include payouts over several years. The purpose of a payout is for the buyer to spread out payments while confirming that the business can sustain or improve its performance. If your payout is tied to future financial results, you will have a strong interest in the company performing well.

If there is a payout period, do everything you can to ensure the transition runs as smoothly as possible. Engage important clients and connect them to the new team. Stay involved in these key relationships to smooth any bumps in the road. This extra effort may ultimately put more money in your pocket.

Next!

When the deal is done, there's one last step: Celebrate – professionally, emotionally and financially!

> Building a business from the ground up to the point where it can be sold is a brilliant accomplishment. Savor the moment.

As the dust settles, consider what comes next. Will this accomplishment launch your retirement, fund a two-year sabbatical, or kick-start your next entrepreneurial venture?

Whatever you decide, make sure to be disciplined and responsible with your new wealth. Understand what your financial future looks like before you take a trip around the world or commit to building an extravagant new home.

On an emotional level, you may experience an adjustment period as you balance your newfound freedom and uncertainty around what to do next. This is a normal transition, experienced by both business sellers and retirees.

The post-paycheck era

Your financial transition may be similar to retirement as well. Instead of funding your lifestyle from your business, you will need to rely your portfolio to do this job for you.

Make sure you build a diversified portfolio with an appropriate risk and return profile for your situation and goals. Diversification is critical. Follow this wise adage in wealth management: "Get wealthy through one company. Stay wealthy through many."

Unless you plan to return to work, the proceeds of your sale may constitute the bulk of your nest egg. How long it lasts depends on the income produced by your investments and your level of spending. Consult your financial advisor to determine where you stand.

Whatever your goals may be, take the time to celebrate and enjoy this next phase of your life.

For more information about living without a paycheck, see Chapter 6, "The Day You Stop Going to Work."

6

The Day You Stop Going to Work

Prepare for retirement – financially and emotionally.

When you're 30, the transition to retirement sounds pretty simple: Stop going to work and enjoy yourself. But as retirement gets closer and closer, it can look much more complicated, even stressful.

Retirement marks more than a career milestone; it also creates big financial, emotional and lifestyle changes. This chapter considers some of the most common issues faced by individuals and couples before, during and after retirement.

Number, Please

The financial industry loves ratios, benchmarks and performance metrics. But ultimately there's one key number that matters more than all the others:

> How much money do you need to comfortably enjoy the rest of your life?

As a financial advisor, this is a question that comes up all the time. I find most people don't really have any idea how much money they'll need, or even how to figure it out. Fortunately, it's a number we can calculate pretty quickly.

Start with spending

What are you currently spending each year?

While most people envision spending less as they get older, research shows that most retirees continue to spend at or near pre-retirement levels. With more free time to devote to hobbies, recreation, grandkids and travel, most 70-year-olds spend like their younger selves.

To determine what you're spending now, simply take the amount you earned last year and subtract income taxes and savings. What's left is what you spent.

For example, if you earned $100,000, paid $22,000 in income tax, and put $10,000 into savings and investments, that means you spent $68,000. This is a good guide for what you'll need in today's dollars for each year of your retirement.

Calculate sources of cash flow

What sources of income will you have during retirement (excluding investments)?

Will you have a pension or receive Social Security benefits? Will you continue to work part time? Do you have rental property that generates cash? Will there be any other income coming in?

Total up these projected cash flow streams. The result reduces the amount you'll need to draw from your portfolio during retirement.

In the example above, if your pension and Social Security total $28,000, that means you'll need an additional $40,000 per year to reach $68,000 and maintain your current standard of living.

So how much do you need in investments to produce that $40,000 each year?

Apply the four percent rule

The four percent rule states that roughly four percent of a well-balanced investment portfolio can be withdrawn annually over a long period of time without severely depleting the principal.

Therefore, if you require $40,000 of cash flow from your portfolio each year, you should have $1,000,000 in investments at the time you retire. (40,000 is four percent of 1,000,000.)

Drilling Deeper Into Your Number

The simple calculations on the previous pages are just that, simple. Using your current spending as a projection for your retirement spending, we came up with a ballpark figure for your future cash flow requirements.

As the disclaimer goes,
your actual results may vary.

Your spending may increase as you age, especially related to healthcare. Long-term care can be very expensive, and long-term care insurance is not cheap either. Depending on your general level of health, family history and lifestyle, you may want to factor in higher healthcare spending in your later years.

Likewise, if you plan to move to a retirement community, this may be more expensive than staying in your home. Your actual costs will vary with the level of services, care and luxury that the community provides.

On the other hand, you may have a more modest retirement in mind, with more time spent at home than traveling. Perhaps you plan to move to a less expensive home, or even live with one of your children.

Some expenses may go away as you get older. For instance, you may reach the landmark of making your last mortgage payment.

All of these factors will influence the burden on your investment portfolio to generate income. Discuss them with your financial advisor.

Ask the computer

Your advisor should also be able to run a computer simulation called a Monte Carlo analysis to provide additional information.

A Monte Carlo analysis runs thousands of future scenarios to calculate the probability of meeting your financial goals.

The beauty of the Monte Carlo software is it acknowledges that the future is variable and uncertain. For instance, your portfolio returns will not be predictable and linear; you may gain 12 percent one year, but lose nine the next.

Because of that variability, the software doesn't spit out one magic retirement number. Instead, the output of a Monte Carlo is a set of probabilities.

The simulation might show an 80 percent probability, for example, that your million dollar retirement portfolio at age 65 will be sustainable through age 85 with a $40,000 annual withdrawal.

It's a very useful tool. Ask about it.

Should I Stay, or Should I Go?

In some career fields, you may not have complete control over when you retire, but even if you do, it can be a tricky decision.

From a financial perspective, keep in mind that your most valuable current asset may be your ability to earn money, either in your existing career or in a new job in retirement.

If you have any question about your nest egg being big enough to last, my best advice is to keep earning and saving. This reduces the pressure on your portfolio to generate cash in future years.

Even if you only work part time, any earnings will help preserve your retirement accounts. Think of it as phasing into retirement, in terms of both time and money.

> If you decide to start a new career in retirement, be realistic about its financial impact.

For instance, pursuing your dream to open a bed and breakfast or café may be extremely rewarding, but it may not meet your income expectations. Remember that most small businesses close within a few years, so be cautious about investing money you will need in the future into an uncertain business opportunity.

Now or later?

Another timing question is when to start receiving Social Security benefits. This is a fairly complicated decision; I won't try to explain it all here. But the basic math is this: The longer you wait to start taking your benefits, the more you will receive each month. So if you can postpone it a few years, you will have more cash flow once you finally start your benefits.

If you don't have the help of a financial advisor to determine the optimal timing to begin your benefits, set up an appointment with the Social Security Administration. They can help you navigate all your options, including survivor and spousal benefits.

Here's Your Allowance

Perhaps the biggest financial adjustment in retirement is being on a fixed income.

While you are working, you can qualify for raises or promotions, change companies, or perhaps work more hours to earn more money. But in retirement, you should think of your cash flow as static – a fixed combination of your pension, Social Security benefits and distributions from investment accounts.

> I encourage you to take a consistent monthly allowance from your investments rather than random withdrawals whenever you need money. This builds the discipline to spend within your means.

If you find your allowance is not lasting through the month, you'll need to consider where you can cut expenses. You may be able to do this simply by paying more attention to how you spend. If awareness alone doesn't close the spending gap, you'll need to put together a budget to provide structure and accountability.

Less house, more cash

An option that helps many people cut expenses is downsizing. The mortgage or rent payments on a smaller home (or one in a more affordable neighborhood) may be less than your current outlay. Maintenance, utilities and taxes may be less, too. In addition, if you sell your current home for a profit, you can add some of that money to your retirement fund.

If you don't have much flexibility with housing and other large expenditures, take a closer look at everyday lifestyle expenses for places where you can cut back.

Maybe it Should be Called "Reset"

Because so many things change at retirement, it's no surprise that some people struggle with the transition.

You may suddenly have more time, less structure and fewer responsibilities.

> This new freedom can be enchanting. Or completely disorienting.

Based on my experience with retired clients, I encourage you to find something you are passionate about and make it a priority. This could be a part-time job, a volunteer cause, grandmother duty, art classes, golf, or anything else that gets you up each day and out of the house.

The key is to stay engaged and involved, even if your new pursuits look nothing like your former career. Your productive years are not ending, just changing.

Challenge yourself to expand your friendships and explore new interests. Join groups for exercise, hobbies and learning. Meet friends for walking, movies or yoga. Set up a book club or take classes at the local college to learn more about your passions. Be a mentor. With more time on your hands, the possibilities are endless.

If your spouse is also retired, think about things you enjoy doing together, but also commit to your own personal interests. This can be a time of adjustment for both of you, so be sure to communicate about shared goals, such as important travel destinations, but give each other space to pursue individual goals as well.

Family balance

It is not uncommon today for retirees to be called upon to care for aging parents, assist adult children or help with the care of grandchildren. These family demands can be both rewarding and stressful.

Either way, they can get in the way of the "dream retirement" that you may have envisioned. Think about how best to balance family obligations with the time you need to enjoy your own interests, even if it sometimes means politely saying, "No."

Retirement is also an ideal time to simplify your financial life:

- Merge multiple 401k plans and other retirement accounts
- Make sure your will and estate planning documents are up to date
- Discuss your financial situation with your children
- Donate work clothes and other items you no longer need

7

Life Does Go On

Find your footing after the death of your spouse.

If you are reading this chapter because your spouse has died, let me offer both my condolences and my encouragement. No matter how much grief, confusion or worry you feel today, my experience working with women who have lost their spouses tells me that you will find your way through this dark time.

Financial matters may seem unwelcome and overwhelming when you lose your spouse. This chapter will help you understand your situation and take positive steps forward.

The Ultimate Question

According to the U.S. Census Bureau, the average age of a new widow in the United States is 55 years old.

For many women, this is a shocking statistic. We typically think of widowhood occurring well into retirement and grandparental years. However, life's transitions can come quickly and unexpectedly.

Recently, I met with a 41-year-old woman I'll call Melissa. Her husband of eighteen years had died suddenly of a heart attack. During our first conversation, she expressed fear about whether she would survive financially.

Will I have enough money?
This is the question I hear most.
It's also one that many
widows can't answer.

Even though Melissa paid the monthly bills and knew how much was in her checking account, she had no idea whether she was financially secure or what her future held when it came to money.

She didn't know what funds were available to support her and her children, or how she would pay the massive college bills that were sure to come.

She didn't know if assets such as her husband's retirement account would be accessible right away, or years in the future.

She didn't know if her investments would last only a few years or the many decades she expected to live.

This scenario is not unusual. I believe Melissa's situation of knowing a lot about one part of the finances and nothing about the rest is typical for couples who often divide responsibilities and conquer them independently.

It was my privilege to help Melissa understand where she stood financially and to build a plan that made sense for her and her children. The following pages describe the process I worked through with her, and the steps I suggest for you if you have lost your spouse.

Find Your Support Team

Dealing with the death of a loved one is difficult, and no one should have to do it alone.

Entire books have been written on the grieving process; this chapter can't replace the detailed insights they contain, and I'm definitely not a psychologist. Even with that disclaimer, I know this: It's very important to have a couple people you can really rely on through this difficult time.

Think of a close friend who can support you emotionally, someone who can be there to listen and lend a hand. I suggest a friend rather than a family member as your first line of support, because close relatives may be experiencing their own grief, or may be influenced by other family relationships or issues. A friend can often be more available and less emotional in lending support.

Just as important, a trusted advisor – a professional with practical experience in the situations you may encounter – will be of great help. A financial advisor, for instance, can help you sort out where you stand and present suggestions on what to do or avoid.

Take Stock of Where You Are

Though it may be the last thing on your mind, understanding your financial situation should be a priority in the months after the death of your spouse.

Before making any major decisions, it is important to first assess your current financial situation. Your friend or advisor, or possibly both, can be helpful with this task, which may require digging around in files, making phone calls and accessing online accounts.

You can think about this as similar to what experts advise for anyone lost in the wild:

> Fully assess what resources you have available before making any decisions or charging off into unknown territory.

Assets

Before you worry about years in the future, make sure you have enough readily accessible cash to keep all bills current (mortgage, car payment, utilities, etc.). The last thing you want to deal with is a call from the bank or having your electricity turned off.

Once immediate bills are covered, do a more detailed inventory of checking, savings, brokerage and retirement accounts.

You may also be entitled to insurance proceeds. These generally require submission of a death certificate or other documents.

Eventually you'll need to make contact with all of the financial institutions where you hold accounts, but start by making a single list of all accounts and financial assets – where they are and what they contain.

Expenses

On the other side of your ledger are expenses, both scheduled payments, such as mortgage and utilities, and everyday expenses like food and clothing.

Make a list of all recurring payments, including when and how they are currently paid (by mail, automatic deduction or online bill pay).

If new expenses such as tuition payments will be starting soon, record those as well.

Creating this type of inventory provides a rational understanding of where your money is and how much you'll need available each month. It's a great starting point for determining how to best move forward.

Look Forward With a Budget

All transitions create change. After the death of a spouse, income may be lost and expenses may rise or fall.

> A budget is an important tool to determine how your cash flow will look in your new reality.

Start by asking yourself the following questions:

- How will my income change?
- What responsibilities do I have for other family members, including children still at home or away at college?
- Which expenses will increase, decrease or go away entirely?
- Will I have new expenses (for example, paying a lawn care company to do yard work my spouse had handled previously)?

Once you have these details, you can build a budget to give yourself an idea whether your current living situation is sustainable or if changes need to be made.

For more detail on budgeting, see Chapter 10, "Where Spending and Saving Meet."

Plan for the Long Term

If you and your spouse had a long-term financial plan in place, it will need revision to reflect your new situation.

If you do not already have a plan, developing one should be a priority.

Either way, you'll need to think carefully about your short-term and long-term goals for yourself and your family.

Think about how you want the next phase of your life to look. Will you want or need to work? Will you quit your job to stay home with your children? How will you spend your time? Where will you live? Will you still use the vacation home or country club membership your spouse loved so much?

These decisions can have a big influence on your cash flow requirements. If your current investments and other sources of income cannot sustain your desired lifestyle, it's best to determine this early so that changes can be made promptly.

Invest in Yourself

Your long-term plan will set the tone for your overall investment strategy.

If you don't have a lot of experience with investing, trying to manage your portfolio yourself can be perilous. Do-it-yourself investors, even those who do have experience, are prone to mistakes that can be very costly. If possible, I suggest you work with a financial advisor to avoid common pitfalls and make the process more productive.

Your focus should be to consolidate and simplify your various accounts and investments and work with your advisor to develop a cohesive plan that fosters the goals you've set for your future.

Keep this in mind: There's no such thing as one ideal portfolio that's right for everyone.

Your portfolio should reflect your specific situation and personal goals. The actual investments you own may be quite different from those of other people you know. Still, there are several fundamental investing principles that your advisor should advocate and pursue:

- Stay invested for the long term
- Diversify holdings across many different stocks and bonds
- Utilize the benefits of tax-advantaged accounts, such as IRAs, where appropriate
- Create a portfolio that provides enough risk to generate the desired return

A well-constructed plan does not require constant tinkering; however, it is important to revisit it on a regular basis and stay accountable to your budget.

You can do it

Nothing in this chapter is particularly difficult, but trying to accomplish it amid the emotional upheaval of the death of your spouse can feel overwhelming.

I encourage you to take small steps and never hesitate to ask for help from your support team along the way.

For more detail on investing, see Chapter 12, "Every Dollar Has a Job to Do."

8

Balancing Loss, Gain and Responsibility

Be a respectful steward of inherited assets.

Inheritance is a tricky thing. It represents both gain and loss at the same time. In receiving an inheritance, you may feel a mix of sorrow, grief, nostalgia and gratitude. You may even feel guilt as you move on without your loved one.

When it comes to inheriting money, investments or property, I've seen many clients struggle to overcome these conflicting emotions. This chapter will help you sort out your emotions and make sound financial decisions after a personal loss.

It's Your Money

It is natural to feel both gratitude for an inheritance and pressure to be a worthy steward of the money.

The money may put you in a different financial position and open new doors for you. It may allow a move to a better neighborhood, more advantages for your children, or the opportunity to change careers.

But with all this possibility comes concern that you will make a mistake with the funds, or make decisions that your loved one might not agree with.

It may take time to accept this idea, but inherited assets are yours and yours alone.

Unless the bequest came with specific conditions, you have complete latitude to spend, save, invest or give away the money as you see fit.

If you receive investments, such as stocks or mutual funds, you can hold or sell them, and do what you want with the proceeds. Don't feel tied to an investment strategy or portfolio that doesn't match your needs.

Remember that the money was left to you to make your life happier and more secure, not to create stress and worry.

You may want to ask yourself what your loved one intended for you and the money, but ultimately you must put yourself first.

Determine what is best for you and your family.

Back to Basics

Inheriting money or investments can be confusing and intimidating. Take a deep breath before you make any big spending or investing decisions. If you're not sure what to do, it's fine to park money in a low-interest savings account while you sort out your options.

Reassess your goals

As with any significant change in financial situation, an inheritance may alter your long-term goals.

> Think about what is most important to you and determine how the new money will help.

Perhaps you had hoped to retire early, go back to school or buy a new home, but money always stood in the way. With the inheritance, you may now have the financial security to pursue those goals.

Or, you may decide to simply add the money to your nest egg and enjoy the benefits when you retire.

Make a new plan

When you've decided on your goals, take some time to plan how you will get there.

The first step is always to review your current financial situation. As you do this, think about how your new resources have changed your situation and expanded your options.

If you have a mortgage, student loans or other debts, consider paying off some or all of them to reduce future cash flow needs. In general, it's best to pay off debts with the highest interest rates first.

If you've not made much progress in saving for retirement, or hope to retire early, consider investing the inheritance with the goal of long-term growth. Utilize tax-advantaged accounts like Individual Retirement Accounts (IRAs), so that you can keep more of the investment return.

If you are already in good shape financially, think about spending a little now and saving the rest for something special in the future.

Better yet, consider giving money to people or causes you believe in.

As you create your plan, remember that any money you expect to spend in the next few years should be held as cash in a savings or money market account. Money for long-term goals can be invested in a portfolio of stocks and bonds.

One Basket. Too Many Eggs.

If you receive an inheritance in the form of investments, you'll face a big decision: hold or sell.

Your choice could have a huge impact on your long-term financial situation, especially if most of the money is concentrated in one or two stocks.

Let's say your favorite uncle Kevin, who worked his entire career at ExxonMobil, leaves you thousands of shares of his employer's stock.

Should you honor Kevin's legacy by keeping all the shares? Or should you liquidate the stock and make other investments? Would selling be an insult to Kevin and his long career?

Many financial decisions are open to debate, but this one, in my opinion, has a clear answer: Sell most or all of the stock.

Spread the risk

The recommendation to sell has nothing to do with my opinion of Exxon or the oil industry, nor is it about your feelings toward your uncle. Instead, it is based on one of primary pillars of investing: *diversification.*

Diversification means spreading assets across many companies in different industries and geographies.

Diversification limits exposure to any one company's stock, which could fall sharply in value due to a failed product, natural disaster, lawsuit or other negative surprise.

Selling the Exxon stock and buying a globally-diversified mix of stock and bond funds will greatly diminish your level of risk versus having all your money tied to one company.

How great is this single-stock peril? Ask anyone who had all their money in Bank of America, one of the world's biggest and most recognizable bank brands, when the financial crisis hit in 2008.

Bank of America lost about 90 percent of its value in the crisis, and has regained only about 20 percent of that loss as of this writing. (Other companies fared far worse, like Lehman Brothers, which disappeared altogether.)

Meanwhile, the S&P 500, an index of the 500 largest U.S. stocks, fell a lot, but far less – 60 percent – during the crisis. Since then, it has not only reversed all of the loss, but has gained an additional 30 percent as of this writing.

There are many ways to honor your uncle's memory, but holding onto his employer's stock needn't be one of them. Go ahead and sell the stock and spread your assets across many large and small companies around the globe.

Don't Spend it Before You Have It

In the movies, the family patriarch dies on Monday, the will is read on Wednesday, and his daughters drive off as millionaires on Thursday.

That's not how it happens in real life.

> Transitioning an estate can be very complicated and time-consuming.

As an heir, the first step is to determine what you are actually receiving – life insurance proceeds, retirement accounts, investment accounts, real property or something else.

Each category of assets has its own rules, transition process and timeline.

For assets that have a beneficiary designation (e.g., retirement accounts or insurance policies), the transition can be relatively easy.

For checking, savings and investment accounts, you may have to first transition the accounts through the estate. The executor of the estate will handle all the movements and transfers of these assets. This may take months. Death certificates and letters of testamentary will be needed to transition any account.

If there is real estate involved, it will need to be retitled through the estate attorney and the probate process. If you choose to sell the property it may take a considerable time to get it on the market and find a buyer ready to pay a favorable price. In other words, don't expect to turn a house into cash overnight.

No matter what kind of asset you are receiving, expect some delays and confusion. Even the best-designed estate plans can hit detours. The transfer of a family business can be especially complicated.

Discuss the timing of any transfer with the executor, and – most importantly – don't spend money before you have it.

Death and Taxes

As in seemingly any aspect of adult life, taxes can be a factor in inheritance.

There could be tax costs associated with selling investments or property. Make sure to consult your financial advisor or tax accountant to determine the consequences of liquidating various assets.

If you are inheriting a tax-deferred account, such as an IRA, be cautious of triggering a big tax liability by distributing its contents.

The proceeds from such a distribution will typically be taxed as ordinary income. This may bump you into a much higher tax bracket, dramatically reducing what is left for you to spend or invest.

Fortunately, most inherited tax-deferred accounts can be rolled into a tax-deferred account in your name. This is an ideal situation, allowing you to avoid paying tax on the balance and maintaining some or all of the tax advantages going forward.

Remember, you may be required to take annual distributions from an inherited tax-deferred account.

Talk to the executor, estate attorney or tax accountant to determine the cost basis of the assets you receive. This will arm you with the information you need to make the best decisions going forward.

Protecting the Proceeds

Eventually, after all the estate's legal work, distributions and transactions are complete, you will receive your inherited assets. You should then take care to ensure you retain control over them as your loved one intended.

If you are single, this is pretty straightforward, but if you are married, you will need to consider whether any new money goes into your name only, or into a joint account with your spouse.

In a community property state (as Texas is), inheritance is considered separate property. In order to keep it as separate property, there are specific rules you need to follow related to the titling of accounts and treatment of any income earned on the assets going forward.

> If you want to keep inherited assets as separate property, they must go into an account in your name only.

Real property should be titled in your name only as well.

I highly recommend keeping all inheritance separate, regardless of how happily married you are. The assets are yours and should stay yours, no matter what your future holds.

Consult your advisors to make sure you treat inherited assets properly.

Pay it Forward

Any large inflow of money creates many options for its use, including giving some of it to people you care about or causes you believe in.

However, there are important factors to consider before making those gifts. First, confirm whether you will still be able to achieve your own personal goals.

For instance, it would be wonderful to use your inheritance to pay for college for all your nieces and nephews. However, if doing so leaves you with a shortfall in your own retirement savings, you may need to scale back your giving. (Paying for even one year of college is still a tremendous gift!)

The tax on generosity

As you make these decisions, be sure that you keep taxes in mind. Under current tax rules, you can gift $14,000 tax-free per recipient, per year. Any giving beyond this amount may require a gift tax return to be filed.

Fortunately, tax laws exempt more than five million dollars in giving from the gift tax over your lifetime. So you would have to give away quite a fortune before you started paying tax on your generosity.

Consult your advisor or a tax professional to make sure the gifts you are making will not cause any current or future tax surprises.

The Next Generation

A final note on inheritance: Think about your own heirs and review your will in light of your newly acquired assets.

Your current will may bequeath all your assets to your spouse. If the inheritance you received is from your family, you may want it to pass directly to your children or other family members instead of to your spouse.

You should ask yourself what the money means to you and who you would like to benefit from it in the future.

Make sure your will reflects these wishes. Updating your will may be as simple as adding a codicil to your current document, specifying to whom an account goes. Or, it may be worthwhile to update your entire will to take into account your new situation.

As I've stated many times in this chapter, I encourage you to seek professional guidance on these matters. It would be a shame to diminish the impact of any inheritance due to a legal oversight or tax misstep.

Money 101

9

Help Your Finances Age Gracefully

Check your financial timeline.

This chapter distills a lifetime of financial priorities down to a few pages. It lists issues, actions and decisions that should be on your radar screen each decade, from your 20s to your 70s. Your financial life may not follow this exact timeline, but it's a place to start.

Find your decade (or your mother's or daughter's) and make sure you're on the right track.

People Mature. Priorities Change.

When I was working on this book, a friend asked me what it was about. I almost answered with something like, "Making smart decisions about money."

But I caught myself. That's not quite it.

> This book is about women and money, not the other way around.

Many of the chapters relate to transitions women face – getting married, raising kids, retiring – and the financial issues that may arise during those transitions.

I organized the book around transitions because just as our personal relationships and roles evolve over a lifetime, so does our relationship with money. Your mindset about money as a 55-year-old mother running a business won't be the same as it was when you were 22 and trying to juggle rent, car payments and student loans.

Use this timeline to understand where you are today and prepare for what lies ahead.

Your 20s

- ***Economize.*** As you start your career and go out on your own, you'll begin to learn the value of a dollar. Be thoughtful when it comes to money. Don't overspend on a bigger apartment or fancier car than you need.
- ***Pay down debt.*** As a new college graduate, you may have credit card debt or student loans. Set up a plan to pay off debt over time, focusing on the highest interest rate debt first. Build the payment plans into your monthly budget.
- ***Avoid new debt.*** Having access to credit provides newfound freedom to make purchases, but be careful. Think hard about new purchases – are they really things you need?
- ***Establish good credit.*** Now is the time to focus on establishing a good credit record. Pay all outstanding debt on time, every time. Doing so helps to build a strong credit rating that will be important for the rest of your life.
- ***Start saving.*** The easiest way to start your retirement savings is by enrolling in your company's 401k plan. Take advantage of the structure set up by your company and the possibility of company matches. If you don't have that option, open an IRA and contribute regularly.
- ***Automate other savings.*** Set up a savings account that you can use for special purchases or short-term goals. Make savings automatic by scheduling regular transfers from your checking account as soon as you are paid.
- ***Manage your raise.*** When you get a raise, don't automatically increase your spending. Be thoughtful about the additional money coming in and how it could help you

the most. Increase your savings before increasing your spending. At a minimum, split the difference – if you get a four percent raise, allocate two percent to savings and allow yourself to enjoy an extra two percent in spending.

- ***Prepare for emergencies.*** Now that you are on your own, you need to prepare for the unknown. Anything can happen to your job, health or family. Build an emergency fund of three to six months' cash flow. This should cover you in the event the unexpected occurs and will give you time to get back on your feet.

Your 30s

- ***Pay off debt.*** Other than holding a mortgage on your house, work hard to pay off any remaining debt. If you have lingering student loans or credit card debt, focus on paying them off as soon as you can.
- ***Create a plan.*** Consider what you want your future to hold. Focus on your short-term and long-term goals and start building a financial plan to reach them.
- ***Talk about money.*** If you're married or have a partner, start the conversation about money and what it means to you. Understand each other's trigger points when it comes to finances and be prepared to compromise on money matters. Take the time to have this conversation before problems arise.
- ***Teach your children.*** It is never too early to start teaching your kids about money. Start by using simple examples to teach lessons about money, especially on the importance of saving for the future.

- ***Increase your savings.*** Be disciplined about increasing your savings every year, even if it's by a small amount. Contribute more to your retirement accounts and put aside money for investments and short-term goals.
- ***Diversify.*** As your savings grow, your investments become more important. Make sure you are investing in a diversified way – stocks and bonds, large and small, domestic and international.
- ***Get life insurance.*** If you have children or assets that need protection in the event of your death, consider the need for insurance coverage. Look at term insurance to cover the period of time you are at risk. Avoid insurance products that combine insurance and investments.

Your 40s

- ***Invest outside your 401k.*** If you haven't already done so, start building an investment portfolio independent of your company's retirement plan. Putting away the IRS maximum for your retirement plan may not be enough to cover your actual retirement needs, so make regular deposits into non-retirement investment accounts.
- ***Plan for college.*** As your children get older, it is very important to start saving for their college education. The more you save for them now, the less you (or they) will have to borrow later. Consider opening a 529 plan or other tax-advantaged education account. Saving for college is important, but don't put it ahead of your own retirement savings.

- ***Revisit goals.*** Goals change over time and plans need to be adjusted. Every few years, re-examine your long-term goals. Adjust as needed to make sure your financial plan and behavior align with your priorities.
- ***Review your risk.*** As your nest egg grows, make sure the risk level of your investments is appropriate for your current situation. Think about reducing your exposure to stocks a little each decade.
- ***Consider an advisor.*** As your investment balance grows, it might be time to hire an advisor. The advisor can set up or review your plan, or manage your investments as well. Your investment portfolio may now be the largest asset you hold. It's sensible to get professional help to protect it.
- ***Hire a CPA.*** As your finances become more complex, it may be smart to hire an accountant to offer tax advice and complete your returns. Often the savings in taxes will far exceed the fee paid to the accountant.
- ***Create a will.*** Everyone should have a will. This is even more important when you have a spouse, children and assets. Not having a will to dictate where your assets should go can make things very difficult, and possibly contentious, for those you leave behind.

Your 50s

- ***Maximize tax-deferred savings.*** When you turn 50, you are allowed a "catch-up contribution" to your retirement account to make up for years when you contributed less than your maximum. Make sure to take advantage of this provision and maximize the amount you put into your tax-deferred accounts going forward.

- ***Evaluate long-term care.*** There are two ways to plan for long-term care: buy an insurance policy or self-insure. Both can be expensive. Based on your current health, financial situation, age and family history, determine which path would be best for you.
- ***Review your allocation.*** As you approach retirement, take another look at your portfolio. Consider your current investment risk level and reduce as needed.
- ***Check your progress.*** Will your current nest egg and monthly savings levels put you on track for retirement? If not, what adjustments need to be made? You can save more, extend your working years or plan to live on less. Start making those adjustments now; you'll have fewer options once you retire.
- ***Help your parents.*** As your parents age, it may be time for you to step up and help. This may include tasks as small as helping with errands or setting up doctors' appointments. Or it could mean taking on all of their finances. Start by having a conversation to understand where they are today and what kind of help they may need.
- ***Cut off your adult children.*** Your grown children need to stand on their own two feet financially. Listen, encourage and offer advice on how to succeed, but don't support them in adulthood. Your retirement could be put at risk if you continue to pay their bills.

Your 60s

- ***Picture retirement.*** Envision what your retirement lifestyle will look like and what it will cost. Does this match up with the plans you have in place, or are you now thinking of something different? Start fine-tuning the details as retirement nears.
- ***Consider your exit plan.*** Determine how long you need or want to work in your current job. If you aren't ready for full retirement, consider a part-time role or a position with less stress and more enjoyment. Sometimes phasing into retirement is the best approach.
- ***Defer Social Security.*** Wait as long as you can to take your Social Security benefits. Every year you defer your payments, up to age 70, you get an increase in your benefit. The longer you wait, the more your monthly check will be.
- ***Control expenses.*** In retirement, be conscious of your spending and don't withdraw more from your portfolio than originally planned. If money is tight, work to reduce expenses.
- ***Consider downsizing.*** If the cost or effort involved in maintaining your home is too great, consider other alternatives. By downsizing, you may be able to reduce expenses and stress, and give yourself more time and money to enjoy.
- ***Get organized.*** Update your will. Create powers of attorney for your spouse or children to step in if needed. Consolidate your investment accounts. Put your financial records in good order.

Your 70s

- ***Stand on your own.*** We never want to think about what life would be like without our partner, but be prepared. Make sure you are both aware of your financial situation in the event that one of you needs to take over the finances or go at it alone.
- ***Consider gifting.*** If you will leave a taxable estate at your death, or if you have more money than you will ever spend, consider giving funds to loved ones now instead of waiting until you die. They may need it more now than later and you will get the satisfaction of seeing them enjoy it.
- ***Define your legacy.*** Consider how you would like to be remembered and put plans in place to achieve it. Are there special charities you would like to donate to now or through your will? Make this a regular part of your monthly budget if you can afford it.
- ***Ask for help.*** There are times in all of our lives when we need others to lean on. Don't be afraid or embarrassed to ask for help if you need it. Your family and friends love you and will be willing to step in when necessary.
- ***Enjoy yourself.*** It has taken a lot of hard work to get to where you are now. Be thankful, celebrate and enjoy!

10

Where Spending and Saving Meet

Build a budget you can live with.

Creating a budget is a task most of us dread. Nonetheless, trying to operate without one, especially during major life transitions, can yield discouraging or disastrous financial results.

Like it or not, to save for the future, you need to be accountable for your spending today. A budget provides that accountability and helps you look at money with a practical, goal-oriented mindset.

The Pretty Much Painless Budget

Personal and family finances can seem overwhelming, but the math is simple: To build savings for short- and long-term goals, we need to spend less than we make.

A budget provides a basis for informed spending decisions, and encourages discipline in a world where you can buy goods and services with cash, checks, debit cards, credit cards, prepaid cards, PayPal, your phone, online bill-pay and automatic withdrawal.

Just spend less than you make.
It sounds so easy.

And it can be. I've found that breaking the big budget monster into five smaller pieces makes the process much easier.

1. Review your spending

The easiest place to start is with what you already know. Look at your last six months of spending to determine where your money goes. Divide expenditures into major categories – including housing, healthcare, clothing, food, car and travel.

Make sure to include every way you spend money – checking account, credit cards, and cash – so you don't miss anything.

2. Break spending down into discretionary and non-discretionary expenses

Not all expenses deserve the same priority. Separate spending on needs, like mortgage, health insurance and food, from optional wants, such as entertainment, recreation and travel.

In the non-discretionary category, remember to include some money for unplanned but necessary expenses, like home and auto repairs.

3. Include a line for savings

Instead of hoping to save what you have left over at the end of each month, be proactive and create a line item for savings. Target ten percent of your income for savings, more if you can.

I strongly encourage you to make saving easy and automatic. Set up a monthly transfer from checking to savings. Schedule it right after payday, so the money moves to savings before you have a chance to spend it.

Create separate accounts for short- and long-term goals and make saving a permanent part of your budget.

4. Reduce unnecessary spending

Once you have logged all your past expenses and your line item for savings, compare the monthly total with your sources of income – salary, alimony, Social Security benefits, retirement accounts, investments, or some combination thereof.

Then take a step back and see what the numbers tell you.

Are you running a deficit? If so, where can you cut back?

Do discretionary items represent a large portion of your monthly spending? Consider cutting back on daily coffee runs, cooking in instead of eating out, or giving up gym or other memberships that go unused. Eliminate some movie channels or cut the cord on cable altogether.

These small spending reductions can add up to big dollars. Attention to discretionary spending can close up your budget deficit or free up more money for savings each month.

It may be more difficult to quickly reduce non-discretionary spending. But if your budget is in the red, all spending should be on the table, even if it means moving to a smaller home or less costly neighborhood.

5. Track, review and adjust

Making your budget is the first big step, but it is not the end of your journey. Make sure to track your actual spending against the budget numbers you've set for yourself.

Things do change over time, so make adjustments as needed, but try to be disciplined and stay true to your goals.

If your children or other loved ones do some of the spending in your household, make sure they understand the limits you have set for different categories. Everyone involved must be informed and accountable for his or her spending.

If you can't make the numbers work, talk to your financial advisor.

How are you doing?

Here's an easy reality check on your budget:

Monitor your credit card balances.

If you're charging more than you can pay off in full each month or have to dip into savings to pay your bills, your budget needs more work.

Best Budget Behaviors

The numbers in your budget are important, but so are your decisions and actions. Follow these tips to increase the chances for success with your budget:

Pay yourself first. Set up automatic drafts from checking to savings as soon as you are paid.

Keep special-purpose accounts. Set up savings accounts for short-term goals. For instance, if you have a $5,000 annual travel budget, you should be saving $400+ per month in a travel account. Having the separate account will remove the temptation to spend that money on other items.

Pay with cash. We have become a credit-dependent society, with painful results for many families. Get in the habit of paying cash for discretionary items so you don't find yourself with a large, unwanted credit card bill at the end of the month.

Pay off high-interest debt. If you have debt from student loans, car loans or credit cards, check the interest rates. Set up a plan to pay off the highest interest rate debt first. Be diligent about payments each month and celebrate as each debt is paid off.

Build your emergency fund. Having an emergency fund of three to six months of living expenses provides a safety net if your income is disrupted. This fund can help in tough circumstances without blowing your budget or building up credit card debt.

Why Budgets Fail

This is not a very encouraging headline, but it's worth discussing. Like diets and exercise programs, many budgeting efforts fall short of expectations. Being aware of the chief reasons why may help you stay on track.

Unrealistic numbers. This seems obvious, but it's a common pitfall. Filling the budget with overly optimistic best-case numbers dooms it to fail. If you regularly spend $600 a month on groceries, use that number unless you have a clear plan to reduce it. Simply hoping to spend less won't reduce your bill.

Lack of tracking. It's easy to create a list or spreadsheet of projected expenses and file it under "Forget all about this." Unfortunately, projections alone will have little, if any, influence on actual spending. It's regular tracking that creates accountability. Mark a date on your calendar each month to track your progress.

Failure to communicate. Money is one of the most common subjects of family disagreements.

> Some families avoid the tension by simply not talking about money at all. This can lead to uncontrolled spending and quick abandonment of the budget.

Omitting one-time costs. You'll have no trouble setting budget numbers for regular monthly expenses like cell phone and cable. But it's not so simple for infrequent events like vacation travel, or unplanned expenses like home repairs. Nonetheless, these are real expenses that can quickly add up. Think about what you've spent on things like this in recent years and take an average. Even a guess is far more realistic than a zero.

Ignoring the cost of daily life. There's a good reason every article on budgeting mentions how a daily Starbucks run adds up to a big annual expense – it's true. Be sure to include, and look for ways to reduce, habitual purchases – coffee, soft drinks, snacks, lunch, wine, bottled water, and so on.

11

Save for a Rainy Day (and Sunny Days, Too)

Make saving part of your routine.

Saving for retirement is like wearing sunscreen. It's easy to forget, you need to do it your whole life, and the benefits may be hard to recognize until you've done it regularly for decades. But if you make a habit of it, it can literally save your life.

Here are some tactics to make saving less of a chore.

Save Early. Save Often.

Imagine if you could get paid for doing nothing.

"Where do I sign up?" you ask.

The answer is your local bank. Just open an account, deposit money every month, sit back, and *voila*, it magically turns into more money.

Everyone knows how saving works, but still it's a habit most people struggle to adopt and maintain. The women I encounter in my work who do the best job with saving have a few things in common:

- They start early in their careers.
- They make it a priority every month.
- When their income rises, they increase their savings.
- They don't dip into savings to pay for discretionary expenses.

Of course, not everyone starts saving early. If you are no longer 25 and feel behind the curve when it comes to savings, there's no better time to start than the present.

Even if you are 50 and feel like it's too late, get started anyway. Start small if necessary. That's far better than not starting at all. Put away money every month. In six months you will already start to feel better. Then you can readjust, add more and keep building.

Make it Automatic

Saving is easy when you make it automatic. Set up a regular transfer from your checking account into your savings account as soon as your paycheck is deposited.

Think of this as a payment to your future self.

By routing money straight into savings, you'll never see it in your wallet or in your checking account. So you won't have an opportunity to spend it. Just set up the transfer and forget about it.

Let your employer help

If your company has a 401k plan, be sure to participate as soon as you are eligible. It is smart and easy. The money is taken directly out of your paycheck before you even see it.

In a traditional 401k, money contributed is not considered taxable wages. So in addition to saving for retirement, you reduce your taxes as well.

If the company has a 401k contribution match, make sure that, at a minimum, you are contributing enough to receive 100 percent of the match. If you contribute less, it's like turning down a raise – you are leaving free money on the table.

Let the IRS help

If you don't have a 401k, you can use an IRA to build your retirement savings.

Both traditional and Roth IRAs provide tax benefits. Traditional IRAs reduce your tax bill today; Roths reduce taxes when you retire.

In addition, putting this money aside allows you to lock it in so you don't touch it until retirement. (Considerable penalties apply if you make withdrawals before retiring.)

Like all things tax-related, there are plenty of rules, restrictions and options, so talk to a tax professional about how to maximize your retirement savings.

Let the markets help

Retirement plans and investment accounts typically provide access to many different kinds of securities, including mutual funds that hold stocks, bonds or both. By holding these investments for years or decades, you have the opportunity for significant appreciation in value.

Set up Your Buckets

I like to think about savings as three distinct buckets.

First, build your emergency fund. Everyone should have a cash reserve on hand for unexpected situations.

An emergency fund provides protection if you have a job change or an unexpected health issue.

If you are working, you should have three to six months of cash on hand.

In retirement, this cash reserve may be 12 to 18 months, or more, depending on how conservative you like to be. The cash reserve funds your living needs so you don't have to pull from investments in a down market.

Your emergency fund should be held in cash and easily accessible. Consider a savings account or money market connected to your checking account so you can access it in a hurry.

Second, start your short-term savings. Short-term savings is for anything you will need in the next five years. Think of the items you may have on your current wish list, such as a down payment on a new house, a new car or any other major purchase.

I suggest putting this short-term saving bucket in your investment account where it's not so easy to access and spend. Hold it as cash in your account so it's protected from market downturns.

Third, invest for the long-term. Any amounts not needed within that five-year period should be invested in the market. Savings for retirement, college tuition for your kids or the purchase of a vacation home 15 years down the road need time to grow.

To build value over time, this money should be in stocks and/or bonds. Savings or money market accounts won't produce enough return to fund your future needs. In fact, low interest accounts may not even keep up with inflation.

Consider this bucket part of your investment portfolio and invest it based on your overall financial plan.

For more information on investing for the long term, see Chapter 12, "Every Dollar Has a Job to Do."

What About Debt?

Consumer debt, especially credit card debt, is one of the biggest financial dangers in America today.

You probably know someone who has overspent on credit cards and now has a scary balance that he or she can't pay. It's not a pretty picture. Interest charges and penalties accrue relentlessly, creating a deeper and deeper hole.

It goes without saying that avoiding this dire situation should be a priority. However, if you do have consumer debt, make a plan to pay it off as quickly as possible.

Like the savings regimen described earlier, make payments part of your monthly routine before making any non-essential expenditures.

You should pay as much as you can to reduce your balance. Ignore the amount on your bill labeled "minimum payment due." Paying this small amount will only result in more and more interest, leaving you further behind. Pay as much as you can, even if it means making sacrifices in other areas of your budget.

Once your debt is paid off, take advantage of the discipline you developed and direct those payments to savings, not to increases in spending.

12

Every Dollar Has a Job to Do

Build the portfolio that's right for you.

A fundamental element in the pursuit of the American dream is investing for the future. But what this means and how to make it happen leaves many people confused.

With thousands of stocks, bonds, mutual funds and other investment options to choose from, deciding where to begin can be bewildering. Ultimately, you need to build a portfolio based on your unique needs, goals and risk tolerance. This chapter will get you started.

One Step at a Time

Creating an investment portfolio can be intimidating. I often sense that new clients feel a little lost as they step into unfamiliar territory. I'm not surprised.

> Investing is complicated and there are many more ways to make mistakes than to do it well.

In some ways, it's similar to renovating a house for the first time. Should you meet with the contractor or the architect first? Should you include a decorator now or later? Should you move out or stay put? How do you balance all the decisions and activities to make the project run smoothly and efficiently?

As with any high-stakes project, the best thing to do is to break it down into smaller pieces and ideas.

Start early

Why would I begin this investment discussion with the advice to start early, an idea so basic and obvious that everyone already knows it? Because few people actually do start investing early. It's easy to procrastinate or think of investing as something to do later in life, but the advantages of saving and investing when you are young are too big to ignore. Just do it.

Separate saving and investing

Saving and investing are two different animals. Any money you'll need in the short term should go into savings – such as a traditional bank savings account or money market account – not the stock market. The market is too risky and can be very volatile in the short term.

For example, if you plan to buy a house in the next few years, keep the down payment in a savings account. However, if you are putting money away for retirement or a vacation home far in the future, it should be invested.

> As a rule of thumb, only put money in the stock market if you're able to leave it there for five years or more.

Diversify

Don't put all your eggs in one basket. This well-worn nugget never goes out of style, and for good reason. Diversification typically reduces risk and improves long-term returns. And it's so easy to do.

Use low-cost mutual funds or exchange-traded funds to spread your stock exposure across many companies – large and small, international and domestic. These funds will have hundreds or thousands of stocks, with limited exposure to any one company.

Avoid a portfolio comprised of only a few individual stock holdings. The return potential may be the same, but the volatility you experience with five stocks versus five thousand is likely to be far greater. A diversified mutual fund could reduce the chance of a bumpier ride.

By the same token, build the bond component of your portfolio using a variety of high quality, short- to intermediate-term bonds, or use a mutual fund that holds many bonds.

To further spread out your assets, consider adding in real estate through a well-diversified real estate investment trust (REIT).

Most importantly, don't let any single holding dominate your portfolio.

Stocks and bonds: What's the difference?

A ***stock*** is an actual ownership stake in a company. Stocks are also called equities.

Some companies grow quickly and flourish for decades while others come and go in months. As a stockholder, you participate in the results, good or bad.

Owning stocks provides the chance for relatively big gains, but also the possibility of big losses.

As you'll recall from the financial crisis in 2008-09, the overall value of U.S. stocks fell by about 60 percent, and some companies fell all the way to zero. These huge losses are rare, but are always a possibility with stocks.

A ***bond*** is a debt security. Bonds are also called fixed-income investments.

When you own a bond, you are essentially making a loan to the bond issuer – which may be a company, a municipality or agency, the U.S. government, or other entity.

The issuer uses the money for the duration of the bond, pays you interest on a regular schedule, and, at maturity, returns the principal.

Bonds can have risk. High-yield (or "junk") bonds, in particular, may lose value if the issuer has trouble making interest payments. However, high quality and short- to intermediate-term bonds generally have less risk than stocks. With lower risk, these bonds typically offer lower returns but greater stability.

Getting the Risk Right

Gauge your risk tolerance

Investing is a balancing act – the more risk you're willing to accept, the higher long-term returns you can hope to earn. Too little risk means your portfolio may not keep up with inflation; too much risk means big swings in the value of your portfolio during volatile markets.

> The right mix for you is the one that provides enough expected return to meet your goals, without being so risky that you can't sleep at night.

Can you stomach big ups and downs in the market? Can you leave money invested for many years? If so, your portfolio can be on the more aggressive side – meaning more stocks and fewer bonds.

As you get closer to retirement and need the money for ongoing living needs, you may want less risk – meaning more bonds in the mix.

A relatively aggressive portfolio might be 70 percent stocks and 30 percent bonds. A more conservative investor, holding perhaps 40 percent stocks and 60 percent bonds, would expect lower returns and less short-term volatility.

Stay in balance

Once you've built a diversified and risk-appropriate portfolio, the key is to keep it that way.

As different elements of your portfolio advance or decline at different rates, your 70/30 allocation of stocks to bonds, for example, may drift to 80/20 or 60/40. Get back in balance by selling some of your best performers and spreading the gain across securities that have lagged. That's selling high and buying low.

This process is called rebalancing. It's an important investment practice, but one that many do-it-yourself investors fail to execute.

Control What You Can

Costs

Despite growing regulatory pressure to be more transparent, the financial services industry generates billions of dollars in profits through expenses and fees that are often difficult to see and evaluate.

Because each dollar lost to fees is one less dollar that can compound in value over future years, fees have a big impact on your long-term investment results.

If you are a do-it-yourself investor, be sure to research your costs before making a purchase. If you are investing in mutual funds, make sure they have low expense ratios.

If you work with an advisor, understand her fee structure and avoid paying commissions or loads. Don't assume how she earns her compensation. Ask.

Taxes

Taxes are even more complicated than fees.

Certain types of investments are better held in tax-advantaged accounts, which reduce or delay the taxable income you receive.

For your stock portfolio, avoid high turnover (frequent buying and selling). Turnover may add to your tax bill with every transaction.

Also be careful of short-term gains, which are generated when you sell a security you've owned for less than one year. These gains are taxed at higher rates than long-term gains (securities held for more than one year). Waiting a few extra months to sell may significantly reduce the share of your profit that goes to taxes.

You may also reduce your taxes by selling some holdings at a loss to offset gains on other holdings.

Like I said, it's complicated. I suggest you talk to an investment advisor or accountant to understand what actions may increase or decrease your annual tax bill. It's difficult to undo a tax mistake, so seek help in advance.

Emotions

The biggest mistake most investors make is letting emotions override discipline.

It's extremely important to not tweak and tinker with holdings with every scary headline and big market swing. Remember, investing is for the long term. Buy, hold, rebalance, and let the market work for you. Keep fear, impatience and envy out of the equation.

An advisor can help here, too, acting as a buffer between your emotions and your portfolio.

If you want to "play the market," do so with a very small sum that you are fully prepared to lose, just like you would at a casino.

For guidance on finding an advisor who can help you design a portfolio that meets your needs, see Chapter 13, "Whom Should You Trust with Your Purse?"

Money Myths

1. Cash is smart.

When markets are falling, it may feel safe and smart to bail out and put all your money in cash. The strategy in doing this is typically to wait until things get better, and then buy back into stocks. But going to cash has two failings.

First, you can lose ground to inflation by holding cash.

Second, how will you know when to exit and when to buy back in? To be successful, you have to be right twice. Individuals in a panic typically sell when stock prices have dropped and buy back in when prices have recovered. So by trying to time the market, you will most likely buy back in at higher prices than when you sold, losing the chance to benefit from the recovery.

> That's basically like returning merchandise you bought on sale and then buying it again when it goes back to full price.

Instead of selling when markets are volatile, rebalance to your intended asset allocation.

2. Home ownership is the best investment you can make.

The American dream has always included owning your own home. Owning your residence can be wonderful for all sorts of reasons, but don't count on it for financial security.

A house may not be a great investment. For one thing, a home is an undiversified and illiquid asset. If you need to sell it quickly at some point, you may have to accept a terrible offer. In addition, you cannot sell off individual sections of your house if you are in a crunch for cash.

Second, it can be very expensive just to protect a home's value. Repairs, maintenance, taxes and association fees can add up, not to mention the huge cost of significant renovations.

Finally, home prices are volatile, moving both up and down. There's no guarantee you will make a decent return on a home, no matter how long you own it.

> Buy a home you love, but don't expect it to be your financial savior; it may be the opposite.

3. Saving for your children's college is your top priority.

As a parent, your instinct is to take care of your children above all else, but there are times when you need to put yourself first. This is especially true when saving for your kids' education comes at the cost of your own retirement.

There are many options when it comes to paying for college. Financial aid, work-study programs and merit-based aid can all contribute toward college costs. And, if needed, your children can always borrow money for college. But you won't be able to borrow money to fund your own retirement.

Create a plan that builds a nest egg for retirement. If there's money left over, save that for college, not the other way around.

4. Money buys happiness.

Many studies actually show that money and material possessions do little to boost happiness. In fact, focusing on money can instead cause anxiety about "keeping up with the Joneses" or create an endless cycle of trying to produce a higher and higher income.

Rather than accumulating material goods you may not need or enjoy, I encourage you to invest time and energy into experiences and memories – special events, trips and other adventures with loved ones. That's the real wealth in life.

13

Whom Should You Trust with Your Purse?

Find an advisor you trust with your future.

When it's time to look for a financial advisor, you won't have any trouble finding one. Tens of thousands of people make their living by managing other people's money.

The real challenge is to find the one who's right for you, the one you're ready to trust not just with your investments, but also with confidential details about your finances, family and career.

It's a very important choice.

Finding Your Personal CFO

Your advisor is someone with whom you will share all kinds of sensitive information, rely on in good times and bad, and, quite possibly, work with for decades. In this relationship, trust is essential.

How do you find trust?

Start by asking your friends and family, the people you love and trust the most. Ask whom they have leaned on along the way. Understand the relationship they have with their advisor and see if it matches your needs and expectations. Also reach out to your professional network (accountants, attorneys, etc.) for names of people they know and trust.

Having recommendations is invaluable, but don't take them at face value. Once you have a list, do your research. The advisor's website is a good place to start. Here are some of the questions you'll want to answer:

What role will she play? Investments are just one piece of your financial life. Ideally, you will find an advisor who can do more than invest your money. Look for someone who can address tax and estate planning, insurance strategies, charitable giving and other financial topics related to your family. You'll need someone you can turn to with any financial questions you may have.

What are her credentials? As you will quickly learn, there are many advisors out there hoping to invest your money – but are they qualified? Make sure you work with someone who has experience and professional credentials. Look for a CPA

(Certified Public Accountant), a CFP (Certified Financial Planner) or a PFS (Personal Financial Specialist). These individuals have gone beyond the basics of getting licensed. They've extended their education and experience to include financial planning as well. They will take into account all aspects of your financial life and apply their skills to accomplish your goals, reduce costs and manage taxes.

What kind of clients does she work with? There are many different investors in the marketplace, from young savers to huge university endowments. Look for someone who works with people like you. You don't want to be her biggest or smallest client. Make sure it's a good match.

How experienced is she? Gauge how long the advisor has been working in the industry, and more specifically, how many downturns she's been through. You want confirmation that her philosophy and client relationships hold up in good times and bad. There's simply no substitute for experience.

Is she a fiduciary? This sounds technical, but it's very important. Fiduciary advisors are legally obligated to put your interests first – even ahead of their own – in all situations. Others, including most stockbrokers, are not held to this standard; they can put their own enrichment ahead of yours.

> Fiduciary status means you will be getting impartial, unbiased and independent advice.

How does she get paid? It is important to work with a fee-only advisor. This means she receives no compensation from any source other than a fee from you – typically a small percentage of your account balance each year. Any advisor who receives commissions or compensation for making recommendations has inherent conflicts of interest that should be avoided.

Is her investment philosophy sound? Some advisors pick investments based on the idea that they can somehow predict when a stock or industry will outperform other investments. This stock picking approach sounds appealing, but decades of empirical research, including that of several Nobel laureates, discredit this prediction-based strategy. The research instead supports investing in the market as a whole through asset class funds that diversify risk and provide market-level returns.

Focus on the basics

Look for an advisor who stresses the nuts and bolts of investing:

- Invest in the market for the long term
- Own a mix of stocks – big and small, domestic and international
- Balance your exposure to stocks with a high quality bond portfolio
- Rebalance periodically when allocations are out of alignment
- Don't panic or react when markets decline

Because Money is Personal

Based on your research, narrow down your list of potential advisors and set up meetings with two or three. The meeting is the best place to really get to know the advisor and determine who she is. You will want to verify what you learned in your research, but most importantly, you want to see if you "click."

> Click: The personal connection you'll feel with the "right" advisor is difficult to describe. But you'll know it when you find it.

This is the kind of connection you're looking for:

Feel at home. The office should be comfortable and inviting. It should be a safe and secure environment, a place where you can speak freely without inhibitions.

Tell your story. Look for someone with whom you are comfortable sharing your story, even topics that are sensitive, personal or embarrassing. No matter what you share, you should feel empathy from the advisor, not judgment.

Get educated. Find an advisor who wants to take the time to explain and educate you about investments, financial planning and progress toward your goals. You want someone who is educated, but more importantly, someone who is willing to educate you. The right advisor will make technical information clear and understandable.

Be heard. The most important information in the meeting is coming from you – where you are and where you hope to be. The best advisor will listen to you and not do all the talking.

Ask anything. Your advisor should make you feel at ease and reassure you that there are no "dumb questions." The more comfortable you feel asking questions, the more productive the relationship will be.

Be the center of the solution. The best advisor will invest with purpose, building your portfolio around your specific goals. Your portfolio needs reason and structure and should not be based solely on the potential for the highest return.

The right advisor will make it clear that the relationship is about YOU.

Characteristics to look for in an advisor:

- Trustworthy
- Respectful
- Candid
- Good listener
- Available
- Responsive
- Reassuring
- Positive
- Reliable
- Focused on you
- Organized

Characteristics to avoid in an advisor:

- Condescending
- Egocentric
- Poor listener
- Impatient
- Overly technical
- Does not focus on your goals
- Flippant about what is important to you
- Does not encourage your questions
- Hard to reach

Money and Family

14

I Thought You Paid that Bill...

Communicate your way to financial harmony.

The rich rewards of being in a relationship change your life, but along with those rewards come many responsibilities. One of the most important of those responsibilities is keeping family finances in order.

Money is definitely not a romantic topic, but it is a crucial one for couples to navigate as a team.

Of Love and Money

Finances can be a major source of stress in a relationship. And, by the way, having a lot of money does not provide instant immunity to financial tensions.

> Many couples hope to avert the tension by simply avoiding the topic of finances altogether. Of course, that typically does more harm than good.

It doesn't have to be that way.

What I find in my work with couples is that the stress apparent at the beginning of the process steadily evolves into relief and reward when a couple connects and finds common ground regarding their finances.

Here are some tips for helping you navigate your finances while keeping your relationship strong. Like most things, it starts with communication. Plan a couple of date nights to cover the topics below.

Where are you now?

Even if you have been together for some time, don't assume you and your partner know everything about your combined financial situation.

Start by listing all your assets – from checking and savings to retirement and investment accounts.

Also list all debts, including mortgages, car loans, student loans and credit cards. Talk about your individual credit scores; they can be very important for your financial future.

List insurance policies and medical insurance.

Where do you want to be?

It is rare for partners to have all of the same goals. Share your candid thoughts about the short- and long-term goals you each have. Don't be surprised if your goals don't match perfectly. That's normal. Look for common ground, but be prepared to make compromises along the way.

- What do you hope to achieve, individually and as a family?
- What will your retirement look like, and when will it start?
- What do you want to provide for your children?
- What other dreams do you have that impact your finances?

What's your financial personality?

All individuals relate to money in different ways. Our upbringing and life experiences create unique financial personalities.

Some of us are better spenders than savers. Some of us worry about money. Some of us see wealth as a measure of personal success. Everyone's different.

As you discuss finances, look for clues about your partner's financial personality. This understanding will help you see how your partner may view things when big decisions about money arise.

Work Together

It's not very romantic to think about a couple as a fiscal relationship, but keeping finances in good order requires that both partners do their part.

Divide and conquer

Having one partner handle everything related to money may lead to problems, especially if the other party needs to take over at some point. It's best if both partners have at least some knowledge of all financial matters.

In terms of the day-to-day money duties, I suggest trying to match interests and skills with the tasks at hand. If you're punctual and detail-oriented, you're a good candidate to pay the monthly bills. If you're more of a big-picture person, you may want to focus on long-term planning and investing.

No matter how responsibilities are divided, ongoing communication is essential. Have a finance meeting every few months to understand how things are going. I know, it sounds like a dreary way to spend an evening, but you'll be glad you did it.

Spend less than you make

Without consciously tracking income and expenses, it's very easy for spending to get out of control. I suggest dividing money into a joint checking account for family bills and two separate accounts for individual spending. Watch the balances on these accounts and on credit cards to identify any spending trends that aren't in sync with agreed-upon goals.

Overspending is not a habit that will just go away on its own.

Review your spending on a regular basis so you both understand where things stand.

Take advantage of benefits

With two working spouses, it is important to review the benefits available to each.

If health insurance is better through one employer (economically, medically, or both), take advantage of it. If life or disability insurance is offered, make sure to participate at the level your family needs.

Be aware of other benefits as well, including retirement plans and company matches; paid leave for family events, sick time and vacation; and other services and discounts that may be available through your company's partnerships.

Set up an emergency plan

You never know when the unexpected will happen. Bad things can happen to anyone and they can be very disruptive to your normal financial routine. Even good things like a work promotion that involves a lot of travel can make life more complicated.

Be prepared. Have three to six months of savings on hand to cover expenses in the event of a medical emergency or a change in employment. Also keep a current list of all bank accounts, bills, insurance contacts and passwords.

Make it easy for your partner to take over your financial duties if needed.

Expand your team

The basics of family finances can be managed by you and your partner, but at some point, you'll need help.

As you consider long-term investing, college savings plans, insurance strategies, tax and estate planning, when to start Social Security benefits and other more complex issues, I recommend you talk to a professional.

A financial advisor encounters complicated financial situations every day and has the time and tools to lay out your options and recommend the most advantageous course of action. A good advisor will make your financial life much simpler and less stressful.

Likewise, be sure to involve an attorney and an accountant. An attorney can help with wills, trusts, powers of attorney and other documents that you'll someday be glad you have. An accountant can help with taxes and planning as your financial life gets more complicated.

Celebrate milestones

You will experience financial highs and lows as a couple. Be sure to keep communicating, review and adjust your plan, and celebrate victories like paying off student loans, buying a home and other big steps forward.

For tips on choosing an advisor to help keep your family finances in order, see Chapter 13, "Whom Should You Trust with Your Purse?"

15

When Parental Roles Flip

Be a dependable financial caregiver.

As women, we typically spend our lives caring for people we love – spouses, children, siblings and, in many cases, parents. When these caring situations extend beyond the day-to-day routine of family responsibilities, it can be difficult to know what to do, where to start or what role to take.

This chapter will help you find your way as a financial caregiver.

Roles Change. Love Remains.

Every family situation is different, but I frequently meet women facing new roles as financial caregivers for their mothers. These situations occur for many reasons, including divorce, widowhood or ailing health.

Finances comprise only one element of senior care, but a very important one. The financial help your mother needs may be as limited as keeping up with her bills or as extensive as managing all of her money tasks, including investing, taxes, insurance and more.

Find your footing in new territory

The first step in this transition is to determine how best to approach your new role without robbing your mother of her independence and financial freedom.

Look for ways to provide support and guidance without taking away all of your mother's decision making, unless absolutely necessary. Your goal should be to provide help today where it's needed most, and take on additional tasks over time as her health and other circumstances dictate.

If approached with proper care,
your mother will see your involvement
as a welcome helping hand,
not an intrusion.

Be a Compassionate Over-Communicator

As with any family situation, it is best to start with a conversation. This conversation with your mother may take a few hours, or it may need to stretch over days, weeks or months.

Finances are a very sensitive topic in many families, so this can be an awkward discussion at first. Start by being open and honest. Tell your mother that you are concerned and available to help. It is important to let her know that she is supported and heard, and that her wishes will be taken into account.

Before taking any action, be sure you understand her long-term goals and what she considers important. If her top priority is to live independently for as long as possible, put this goal at the center of your discussion and planning.

> You may think you know what your mother is thinking, but take the time to ask.

Talk about what aspects of her financial situation you will handle, and what she needs or wants to do herself. Your initial role may be as simple as paying bills, or you may need to take the helm on all financial matters. Talk it through so you are both on the same page and your mother feels involved.

When's the right time to have this conversation?

Ideally, you should start the conversation while your mother is in good mental and physical health. Waiting until her health has deteriorated or an emergency has occurred can raise the stress level considerably and reduce your options. If an emergency leaves your mother unable to provide information and discuss her needs, you will be forced to make decisions without all the facts.

Take the time to listen. Be sure to give your mother plenty of opportunity to ask questions of her own.

> Your mother's questions may help you identify any financial problem areas where she needs extra help.

What if your mother won't talk to you about money?

You have many possible avenues to help your mother manage her finances; however they all rely on her sharing information with you.

It doesn't always work out that way.

If she's not willing to open up to you, see if you can bring in a third party – a friend or professional advisor – to facilitate the process. Having an outsider involved may make it easier for her to talk about sensitive information or ease any mother-daughter tensions that could undermine the process.

The goal is to make sure your mother is taken care of – whether by you or someone else.

Peeling the Onion

Your discussion will quickly reveal how many layers comprise a financial life – from income and spending to investments and insurance. Depending on your mother's situation and capabilities, you may need to explore some or all of them. Take your time, and take good notes.

Start with her assets

Make a list of all accounts – checking, savings, investment and retirement.

Determine what other investments she may hold, such as property or an ownership stake in a family member's business venture.

Are there any insurance or annuity policies that she either owns outright or continues to pay on?

Include the value of her house and any outstanding mortgage.

Determine if there are other debts that need to be addressed.

See if she has a long-term care policy and understand the benefits associated with it.

Know where important documents are located and make a list of passwords for online account access.

Find out if your mother has her own network of advisors, such as an attorney, CPA and/or investment advisor. If so, it may be helpful to set up meetings with your mom and her advisors to get a better understanding of her current situation and any financial and legal plans she already has in place.

Determine her budget

Get back to the basics. Understand what income she may be receiving each month from pensions, Social Security benefits or investments.

Do a review of the last three months of transactions to determine what her monthly spending rate is. Also consider non-routine costs she may have, such as property taxes, health care or home repairs.

As you become more familiar with your mother's situation, you will learn if she is having any cash flow problems. If her income is not covering her expenses, see if her portfolio can cover the shortfall.

> It's okay to tap into retirement savings to supplement monthly income – that's its purpose, of course – as long as the withdrawal rate is sustainable.

If supporting current spending is a problem, consider areas where she can cut back. Start with small items she no longer needs – an old insurance policy, or club memberships and subscriptions that she no longer uses.

If you find your mother has a significant cash flow shortfall that is too large to fix by spending less day-to-day, you'll need to take a look at her big expenses, especially housing. That means considering options such as downsizing to a smaller home or apartment. Or, yes, moving in with one of her children.

Set up the bills

Whether your mother likes to write checks once a month or has made the leap to paying online, make a list of all monthly, quarterly and annual bills.

Set up a plan to ensure everything gets paid on time. Automatic withdrawals from a checking account are ideal for utilities and many other bills; they mean less work for you and less worry for her.

Be sure to communicate any changes in how and when bills are being paid so your mother knows what to expect.

Take care of the legal

If you are going to step into your mother's shoes, you will need a legal power of attorney. This document gives you the ability to act on her behalf in all financial matters.

You can utilize the power of attorney for all bank and investment accounts. You will be able to pay her bills, manage her assets and make any financial decisions on her behalf.

The power of attorney is an important tool to have in place. Set it up while your mom is in a good mental state. If you wait too long you may have to deal with a court to establish this authority.

Now is a good time to review her will as well. If it is more than five years old, it may need to be updated. Wishes change over time, so make sure her current thoughts are incorporated. Have a conversation about where she wants her assets to go, including her special personal possessions.

Make sure she has a healthcare power of attorney and medical directive as well.

Manage the investments

Hopefully, your mother has some money put away as a nest egg. If so, understand how it is invested. Determine if her portfolio is diversified, with appropriate balance between stocks and bonds. If changes in cash flow are needed, make sure they are incorporated so the portfolio can support her needs.

> If you have a financial advisor, have her take a look to see if the portfolio makes sense for someone in your mother's situation.

With life expectancies steadily rising, seemingly robust nest eggs can be depleted if withdrawals are too frequent or too steep. A useful rule of thumb is that if you need to withdraw more than four percent of a diversified investment account each year, the portfolio may not last through a long retirement.

A financial advisor can help clarify how long her funds will last, and recommend portfolio changes that may extend the lifespan of her retirement savings.

Keep your money separate

As you become more involved in your mother's finances, be diligent about which accounts you use to pay her bills. To avoid tax and estate problems, make sure not to commingle your accounts with hers.

You may feel a desire to spend your own money to make your mother's life easier or solve a financial problem she has. This instinct is wonderful, however you should be cautious to not spend so much of your money that you jeopardize your own financial future. Help where you can, but don't commit to more than you can afford.

Stay connected

Take time each month, quarter or year to walk your mom through her financial situation. Even if everything is running smoothly, let her know that. If she has the ability to participate and understand, the discussion will reaffirm that she is part of the process and that her input matters.

If you have siblings, let them know what you are doing for your mother so you are all on the same page. If you disagree on what your mother needs, talk through it. Don't let mutual concern turn into a family argument.

Prepare and Adjust

Any change in life circumstances can throw us for a loop, especially as we get older and experience medical issues. If your mother's situation changes due to a decline in health or other big life transition, be sure to revisit her plan and make adjustments as needed.

Think through the tough questions: Will her medical expenses increase? Will she need to consider assisted living? Is home healthcare necessary and affordable?

If her financial situation is good enough to give you the freedom to make any choice, take the time to determine what works best for your mom and for you.

If she doesn't have complete financial freedom, look for healthcare options that balance her needs, desires and budget. Be careful to avoid any choices that would quickly exhaust her savings.

Plan ahead

Making important decisions under time pressure and emotional stress can be daunting.

If possible, consider future care options while your mother is still in good health. You will have more time to explore your alternatives and a clearer mind to make decisions.

Overall, the responsibility of assisting your mother with her finances can feel overwhelming, but take small steps and know that the effort will help your mother live with more confidence and less worry. It's worth it.

16

Feeding the Piggy Bank

Teach your children about money.

Lack of financial literacy is a big problem in America. The average citizen saves too little, spends too much and takes on too much debt. Few people understand even the basics of investing. Because the education system has done so little to help young people build financial knowledge, parents must take the lead.

Whether your child is five or 25, a few key lessons about money will get her started in the right financial direction.

Making Money Real Again

I fondly remember one of the first lessons I learned about money from my father.

I had a savings account where I deposited birthday money and any other funds accumulated throughout the year. I brought my passbook to the bank, and the teller printed in the amount of my deposit plus the interest earned since my last visit.

On one visit, I realized I had earned two dollars in interest. This was big money for an eight-year-old kid in the 70s.

The first thing that came to my mind was to pull out the two dollars and buy milkshakes for my father and me. Of course this became a perfect teachable moment – he took the opportunity to tell me about the importance of saving, interest and letting the money grow for my future.

I guess his lesson worked; I still remember that day all these decades later and I now make a living helping women make good financial decisions. Thank you, Dad!

I'm so glad my parents instilled in me the value of a dollar, and I know parents need to do the same today. But I think my folks had one advantage over today's parents in getting their point across: Back then, money was tactile.

If you were a youngster in the 70s, money was something you actually touched. You saved coins in a pink pig, paid cash for everything you bought, and when you received a monetary birthday gift, it came in the form of a nice crisp five-dollar bill.

Money had volume, mass and texture. Shaking that piggy bank made a joyful sound.

> Today, money is more concept than currency. Like music, money's gone digital.

Most transactions today are electronic, not physical. For birthday celebrations, kind aunts give iTunes gift cards, not cash. Savings account balances live as pixels on computer screens, not as printed numbers in passbooks. Cash comes from ATMs, not tellers.

Teaching kids about conceptual money instead of physical money compounds the challenge that parents face today. It's much harder to attach value to an online account than to hard currency passed from hand to hand.

Money's amorphous form also makes those lessons that much more important; spending hundreds of dollars with the click of a mouse has become dangerously easy.

Money needs to be real in the mind of kids. They need to touch it.

It's Never Too Early

Parents often ask me when to start talking to kids about money.

The answer is right now. Just like saving for retirement, the earlier you start educating your children about money, the better off they will be.

While young children don't need to hear scary stories about missing mortgage payments or running out of money, I encourage you to talk with your kids about earning, spending and saving. Early and often.

For instance, when kids are old enough to help with small tasks around the house, introduce them to the idea that they can do a job and be rewarded with money of their own. Pay them in cash that they can hold, count and accumulate.

If your son earns a dollar for a week of feeding the pets and wants to buy a toy that costs five dollars, he'll soon understand that it takes five weeks of work to buy what he wants.

Tasks like these will put into perspective how much things cost and how much work is necessary to make a purchase.

In our credit card world, this is a lesson people of all ages can use. Learning it young is a valuable bonus for your children.

Save. Share. Spend.

As children begin to see the connection between working and receiving money, it's time to discuss how they will use their money.

Explain to your children that every dollar they receive can be split among three equally important buckets: save, share and spend. Your children can decide, alone or with your help, how to divide up their money.

If you want to reinforce this choice in concrete terms, you can even buy a three-slot coin bank that has separate compartments for these three categories.

> The concept of save, share and spend is really a lesson about priorities and limits.

If your son's first instinct is to spend every cent on games or other goodies, he'll have nothing left to share with others or to save for the future. Conversely, if you can influence (not command) him to prioritize saving and sharing, he'll have to be more selective about what he buys. These trade-offs create invaluable learning moments.

When it comes to sharing, I'm continually impressed by how generous kids can be with their time and money. Young people seem to have an instinct to help others through large and small acts of kindness, an instinct that fades for many people as they get older.

You can encourage this instinct by discussing local charitable efforts, fundraising drives and volunteer activities. The size of their contributions means much less than the big idea of lending a helping hand.

Owe? No.

Most children know all about borrowing and lending – whether it is a pen for math class, lunch money or a soccer ball. If you ask politely and return the item as promised, borrowing is no big deal.

Until paying interest enters the equation.

When you incur debt, some of your future cash flow will have to be used to pay off what you owe.

Furthermore, the amount you repay is not just the amount borrowed, but also the interest charged.

And then the interest on the interest.

And in the case of credit cards, fees for late payments and other sins.

We all know stories of people who have simply spent too much and amassed incredible debt burdens. Most of these stories turn out badly.

At some point before your kids incur any interest-bearing debt of their own – and definitely before they leave your household for college or career – have this discussion.

Explain the monumental difference between using a debit card, where you're spending money you have in your account, versus charging items to a credit card, where you are borrowing money and promising to pay interest for as long as it takes to repay the debt.

Explain that interest works like a snowball rolling down a hill. It grows quickly if it is allowed to get started.

Also explain the importance of establishing good credit. Once your daughter has income, she can build a credit history by using a credit card – sparingly and responsibly – and paying back any other loans on time or early.

This good credit behavior is rewarded not just with lower interest rates on mortgages and car loans, but in many other areas of early adult life. Your daughter's ability to get car insurance, to rent an apartment, even to get a job, may all depend to some extent on her credit score.

The discussion about debt often turns into a dour sermon. That's okay. It's a serious topic. Teach your kids to be patient and thoughtful around spending. Mistakes with credit can really turn a young life upside down.

Avoid the Budget Crisis

Every child's transition into adulthood is different, but at some point (hopefully!) all kids reach the milestone where they make their own money and pay their own expenses.

As parents, we look forward to that day with a mix of pride and concern. Will my daughter spend wisely or develop a shopping addiction? Will my son try to maintain a lifestyle that exceeds his means?

In the end, only your kids can determine their financial fates, but you can teach them some money skills and influence their outlook on spending along the way.

Which brings us to a topic so important to financial well-being that it is discussed in several chapters of this book: budgeting.

Few people like creating a budget, much less sticking to one. But a budget acts like the guardrails along a highway – it helps mark the desired path and limits the damage if you go off course.

> Getting into a budget habit early promotes financial wellness for a lifetime.

To me, budgeting is like planning out personal and family calendars. Every week, my husband and I sit down and talk through what commitments we have – school, the kids' activities and family time. How do we fit all the various time commitments into one week? We juggle, prioritize and sacrifice.

Budgeting is the same. You have a certain amount of money you can spend each month to achieve your goals, manage your lifestyle and save for your future.

Show your kids the process of making choices around money based on priorities. Reinforce the necessity to compromise and sacrifice along the way.

Keep in mind that a variety of websites and mobile apps make budgeting less onerous and even a little bit enjoyable. If these make it easier for your kids to keep a budget, they're worth a look.

For more on budgeting, see Chapter 10, "Where Spending and Saving Meet."

Undo the Taboo

Money can be a very taboo subject.

Most people don't want friends or family to know how much money they make or what they spend it on.

Just the idea of talking about money at the dinner table would make heads spin in many households.

For some, admitting a financial mistake can seem as shameful as failing in school or cheating in a relationship.

> Civilized people just
> don't talk about money.

That's how it's always been, but it needs to change. And you can change it. Here's how:

- Start by sharing information with your kids about your own financial situation, good or bad.
- Talk about your goals, such as paying for college, saving for a secure retirement, or someday buying a vacation home.
- Discuss how you make decisions about money and use a budget to keep you on track.
- Talk about the importance of having three to six months of cash in an emergency fund.
- Explain your own save, share and spend plans. What are you saving for, and whom will your sharing benefit? Let your kids weigh in on these decisions.

- If you are working with an advisor, discuss the kinds of issues she helps you with.
- And be real. Tell your kids about the biggest financial mistakes you've made, such as a big purchase you later regretted, or trusting the wrong person when it came to investing.

It's been my experience that families that ignore the taboo and communicate candidly about money have a much stronger chance of meeting their financial goals. I encourage you to get the conversation started.

I hope that one day my children share these same lessons with their children so the cycle of education and financial responsibility continues.

About the Author

Stuart Vick Smith is a wealth advisor with ML&R Wealth Management in Austin, Texas. The focus of her practice is helping women navigate the often-confusing world of financial planning and investments.

Stuart often works with women who are facing major life events, such as retirement, divorce or the death of a spouse. With emphasis on deep, lasting client relationships, she serves her clients as a holistic planner, not just an investment advisor.

Recognized as a leader in her field, Stuart frequently speaks at local and national events on the topic of women and wealth. She regularly appears on KVUE news in Austin to discuss personal financial topics.

Before Stuart began her role as an advisor in 2005, she worked as a CPA, with an emphasis on taxes. She attended the University of Texas at Austin and the University of Virginia.

Stuart lives in Austin with her husband, two kids and two rescue dogs. When not working, she is either traveling or reading a good book.

For more information and numerous articles and videos on financial planning, visit Stuart's web page: www.stuartvicksmith.com.

For More Information

To order additional books, request a meeting, schedule a speaking engagement, or contact the author, please visit www.stuartvicksmith.com.

For information about ML&R Wealth Management, please visit www.mlrwm.com.